I0006514

INDUSTRY PERSPECTIVES ON THE PRESIDENT'S CYBERSECURITY INFORMATION-SHARING PROPOSAL

HEARING

BEFORE THE

SUBCOMMITTEE ON CYBERSECURITY, INFRASTRUCTURE PROTECTION, AND SECURITY TECHNOLOGIES

OF THE

COMMITTEE ON HOMELAND SECURITY HOUSE OF REPRESENTATIVES

ONE HUNDRED FOURTEENTH CONGRESS

FIRST SESSION

MARCH 4, 2015

Serial No. 114–7

Printed for the use of the Committee on Homeland Security

Available via the World Wide Web: http://www.gpo.gov/fdsys/

U.S. GOVERNMENT PUBLISHING OFFICE

94–578 PDF   WASHINGTON : 2015

COMMITTEE ON HOMELAND SECURITY

MICHAEL T. MCCAUL, Texas, *Chairman*

LAMAR SMITH, Texas
PETER T. KING, New York
MIKE ROGERS, Alabama
CANDICE S. MILLER, Michigan, *Vice Chair*
JEFF DUNCAN, South Carolina
TOM MARINO, Pennsylvania
STEVEN M. PALAZZO, Mississippi
LOU BARLETTA, Pennsylvania
SCOTT PERRY, Pennsylvania
CURT CLAWSON, Florida
JOHN KATKO, New York
WILL HURD, Texas
EARL L. "BUDDY" CARTER, Georgia
MARK WALKER, North Carolina
BARRY LOUDERMILK, Georgia
MARTHA MCSALLY, Arizona
JOHN RATCLIFFE, Texas

BENNIE G. THOMPSON, Mississippi
LORETTA SANCHEZ, California
SHEILA JACKSON LEE, Texas
JAMES R. LANGEVIN, Rhode Island
BRIAN HIGGINS, New York
CEDRIC L. RICHMOND, Louisiana
WILLIAM R. KEATING, Massachusetts
DONALD M. PAYNE, JR., New Jersey
FILEMON VELA, Texas
BONNIE WATSON COLEMAN, New Jersey
KATHLEEN M. RICE, New York
NORMA J. TORRES, California

BRENDAN P. SHIELDS, *Staff Director*
JOAN V. O'HARA, *General Counsel*
MICHAEL S. TWINCHEK, *Chief Clerk*
I. LANIER AVANT, *Minority Staff Director*

———

SUBCOMMITTEE ON CYBERSECURITY, INFRASTRUCTURE PROTECTION, AND SECURITY TECHNOLOGIES

JOHN RATCLIFFE, Texas, *Chairman*

PETER T. KING, New York
TOM MARINO, Pennsylvania
STEVEN M. PALAZZO, Mississippi
SCOTT PERRY, Pennsylvania
CURT CLAWSON, Florida
MICHAEL T. MCCAUL, Texas *(ex officio)*

CEDRIC L. RICHMOND, Louisiana
LORETTA SANCHEZ, California
SHEILA JACKSON LEE, Texas
JAMES R. LANGEVIN, Rhode Island
BENNIE G. THOMPSON, Mississippi *(ex officio)*

BRETT DEWITT, *Subcommittee Staff Director*
DENNIS TERRY, *Subcommittee Clerk*
CHRISTOPHER SCHEPIS, *Minority Subcommittee Staff Director*

(II)

CONTENTS

INDUSTRY PERSPECTIVES ON THE PRESIDENT'S CYBERSECURITY INFORMATION-SHARING PROPOSAL

Wednesday, March 4, 2015

U.S. HOUSE OF REPRESENTATIVES,
COMMITTEE ON HOMELAND SECURITY,
SUBCOMMITTEE ON CYBERSECURITY, INFRASTRUCTURE
PROTECTION, AND SECURITY TECHNOLOGIES,
Washington, DC.

The subcommittee met, pursuant to call, at 2:06 p.m., in Room 311, Cannon House Office Building, Hon. John Ratcliffe [Chairman of the subcommittee] presiding.

Present: Representatives Ratcliffe, Clawson, and Langevin.

Mr. RATCLIFFE. The Committee on Homeland Security, Subcommittee on Cybersecurity, Infrastructure Protection, and Security Technologies, will come to order.

I now recognize myself for an opening statement.

The subcommittee meets today to hear from key stakeholders, including industry, privacy advocates in academia, on the President's cybersecurity information-sharing proposal in recent cyber initiatives.

Last week the full committee heard testimony from the Department of Homeland Security's top cyber officials on the growing cybersecurity threat and how this legislative proposal could enhance protection of our digital networks and American's most personal information.

Today we turn to the private sector and look forward to hearing from our witnesses on what they think cyber threat-sharing legislation should look like. For years, the private sector has been on the front line battling devastating cyber attacks from criminals, activists in nation-states such as Iran, China, Russia, and North Korea. Any cyber threat-sharing legislation produced by Congress should enhance existing capabilities and relationships while establishing procedures to safeguard personal privacy.

Protecting privacy and the integrity of information is what compels us to act. The recent cyber breach of health insurance giant Anthem exposed the personal information of up to 80 million Americans, approximately 1 in every 4 Americans, demonstrating that the quantity and sophistication of these attacks is only increasing.

Just last week the director of national intelligence, James Clapper, underscored this fact, stating that cyber attacks against us are increasing in frequency, scale, sophistication, and severity of impact and that the methods of attack and the systems targeted and

(1)

the victims are also expanding in diversity and intensity on a daily basis.

He emphasized that privacy and the integrity of information are indeed at risk, stating that, "In the future, we will probably see cyber operations that change or manipulate electronic information to compromise its integrity instead of simply deleting or disrupting access to it."

Director Clapper also revealed that, in 2014, America saw for the first time destructive cyber attacks carried out on U.S. soil by nation-state entities when he confirmed that Iran was behind the cyber attack against the Las Vegas Sands Corporation, which is owned by a vocal supporter of Israel. These breaches are now becoming the norm with attacks on Sony Pictures, Target, Home Depot, JPMorgan, and others as evidence of that fact.

FBI director Jim Comey recently stated, "There are two kinds of big companies in the United States, those who have been hacked by the Chinese and those who don't know they have been hacked by the Chinese."

Further, these attacks are not just affecting the largest businesses in financial institutions, but small and medium ones as well. Accordingly, we need to pass legislation that facilitates the sharing of cyber threat indicators and contains robust privacy protections to improve collaboration between Federal civilian agencies, like the DHS, and the private sector.

The Department of Homeland Security's National Cybersecurity and Communications Integration Center, or NCCIC, has been at the forefront of working with the private sector to facilitate cyber threat sharing between the Government and the private sector. NCCIC is a civilian cyber operations center with an embedded statutorily-required privacy office.

In fact, both industry and privacy advocates support NCCIC, which was codified into law last year in bipartisan legislation produced by this committee. NCCIC has been the lead civilian portal for cyber threat sharing between the private sector and the Government, and it is important that NCCIC and other civilian portals be the focus of any cyber threat-sharing legislation.

Today many companies still choose not to share cyber threat indicators with one another or with NCCIC because they fear legal liability. Information about an attack experienced by one company can enable another to fortify its defenses. Yet, when the sharing does not occur, it leaves all of us more vulnerable because the same criminals can use the same tactics to target other companies, exposing even more Americans to having their private information compromised.

Past legislative attempts to improve cyber threat sharing between the private sector and Government and private sector-to-private sector have failed in large part because they could not balance privacy protections with the need for industry to share cyber threat indicators. This Congress I look forward to working with Chairman McCaul, Ranking Member Thompson, and Ranking Member Richmond to craft thoughtful cybersecurity legislation that achieves this balance.

I look forward to hearing from each of the witnesses in their respective fields about the opinions on how best this committee should move forward on drafting legislation to address these issues and what perspectives each of you have on the President's recent legislative proposal and cyber initiatives.

Every generation faces monumental moments where its tenacity to overcome the challenges of our time are tested. Now is our time, as we move deeper into the digital age, to ensure that the cybersecurity challenges we face today are met with the same resolve shown by previous generations of Americans.

I want to thank the witnesses for testifying before this committee, and I look forward to your testimony.

[The statement of Chairman Ratcliffe follows:]

STATEMENT OF CHAIRMAN JOHN RATCLIFFE

FEBRUARY 4, 2015

The subcommittee meets today to hear from key stakeholders including industry, privacy advocates, and academia on the President's cybersecurity information sharing proposal and recent cyber initiatives. Last week, the full committee heard testimony from the Department of Homeland Security's top cyber officials on the growing cybersecurity threat and how this legislative proposal could enhance protection of our digital networks and Americans' most personal information. Today, we turn to the private sector and look forward to hearing from our witnesses on what they think cyber threat-sharing legislation should look like.

For years, the private sector has been on the front lines battling devastating cyber attacks from criminals, hacktivists, and nation-states such as Iran, China, Russia, and North Korea. Any cyber threat-sharing legislation produced by Congress should enhance existing capabilities and relationships while establishing procedures to safeguard personal privacy.

Protecting privacy and the integrity of information is what compels us to act. The recent cyber breach of health insurance giant Anthem exposed the personal information of up to 80 million individuals—approximately 1 in 4 Americans—demonstrating that the quantity and sophistication of these attacks are only increasing. Just last week, Director of National Intelligence, James Clapper underscored this fact, stating that "[cyber] attacks against us are increasing in frequency, scale, sophistication and severity of impact" and "the methods of attack, the systems targeted, and the victims are also expanding in diversity and intensity on a daily basis." He emphasized that privacy and the integrity of information are indeed at risk, stating, "in the future, we'll probably see cyber operations that change or manipulate electronic information to compromise its integrity instead of simply deleting or disrupting access to it."

Director Clapper also revealed that in 2014, America "saw, for the first time, destructive cyber attacks carried out on U.S. soil by nation-state entities," confirming that Iran was behind a cyber attack against the Las Vegas Sands Corp., which is owned by a vocal supporter of Israel.

These breaches are becoming the norm, with attacks on Sony Pictures, Target, Home Depot, JP Morgan, and many others. FBI Director James Comey stated, "There are two kinds of big companies in the United States. There are those who've been hacked by the Chinese and those who don't know they've been hacked by the Chinese." Further, these attacks are not just affecting the largest businesses and financial institutions, but small and medium ones as well. As such, we need to pass legislation that facilitates the sharing of cyber threat indicators and contains robust privacy protections to improve collaboration between Federal civilian agencies like DHS and the private sector.

The Department of Homeland Security's National Cybersecurity and Communications Integration Center, or NCCIC, has been at the forefront working with the private sector to facilitate cyber threat sharing between the Government and the private sector. NCCIC is a civilian cyber operations center with an embedded statutorily-required privacy office. In fact, both industry and privacy advocates support NCCIC, which was codified into law last year in bipartisan legislation produced by this committee.

NCCIC has been the lead civilian portal for cyber threat sharing between the private sector and the Government and it is important that NCCIC and other civilian portals be the focus of any cyber threat-sharing legislation.

Today, many companies still choose not to share cyber threat indicators with one another or NCCIC because they fear legal liability. Information about an attack experienced by one can enable another to fortify its defenses. Yet when this sharing does not occur, it leaves all of us more vulnerable because the same criminals can use the same tactics to target other companies, exposing even more Americans to having their private information compromised.

Past legislative attempts to improve cyber threat sharing between the private sector and Government, and private sector-to-private sector, have failed in large part because they could not balance privacy protections with the need for industry to share cyber threat indicators. This Congress, I look forward to working with Chairman McCaul, Ranking Member Thompson, and Ranking Member Richmond to craft thoughtful cybersecurity legislation that achieves this balance.

I look forward to hearing from each of the witnesses in their respective fields about their opinions on how best this committee should move forward on drafting legislation to address these issues and what perspectives each of you have on the President's recent legislative proposal and cyber initiatives.

Every generation faces monumental moments where their tenacity to overcome the challenges of the time are tested. Now is our time, as we move deeper into the digital age, to ensure that the cybersecurity challenges we face today are met with the same resolve shown by previous generations of Americans.

I want to thank the witnesses for testifying before this committee and I look forward to your testimony.

Mr. RATCLIFFE. Next I will ask for unanimous consent to insert into the record the letters received by the committee from the following organizations: National Defense Industrial Association, American Bankers Association, Retail Industry Leaders Association, and the Financial Services Information Sharing and Analysis Center. Without objection, so ordered.

[The information follows:]

LETTER FROM THE NATIONAL DEFENSE INDUSTRIAL ASSOCIATION

MARCH 3, 2015.

The Honorable MICHAEL MCCAUL,
Chairman, Committee on Homeland Security, U.S. House of Representatives.
The Honorable BENNIE THOMPSON,
Ranking Member, Committee on Homeland Security, U.S. House of Representatives.

DEAR CHAIRMAN MCCAUL AND RANKING MEMBER THOMPSON: The National Defense Industrial Association (NDIA) is a non-partisan, non-profit, association with more than 1,600 corporate members and approximately 90,000 individual members. On March 4, 2015, your committee will hold a hearing titled "Industry Perspectives on the President's Cybersecurity Information-Sharing Proposal." NDIA has received pertinent comments from its membership concerning the President's proposal which I have enclosed with this letter. Below is a synopsis of those comments to inform your committee hearing.

The President's Cybersecurity Information-Sharing Proposal sometimes uses vague language that makes the legislation subject to the reader's interpretation. For example, section 103(c)(2) of the proposal states that a private entity receiving cyber threat indicators shall take "reasonable efforts" to protect the privacy of specific individuals and to "safeguard" information on specific persons. Section 103(c)(3) of the same proposal also uses the term "reasonable." However, the proposal does not define what is "reasonable," or what is adequate "safeguarding." These undefined terms leave the door open for an enforcing agency or court to step in and provide definitions at their discretion, Instead, NDIA proposes that any legislation define what is "reasonable" or where such a definition can be obtained, such as in an industry or Government standard. To that end, we recommend that the work done by the National Institute of Standards and Technology (NIST) expand to include these definitions.

The President's proposal also contemplates the creation of Information Sharing and Analysis Organizations (ISAOs) for the sharing of information by private industry. The role of ISAOs is further explained by Executive Order 13691, "Promoting Private Sector Cybersecurity Information Sharing." Nothing appears to preclude existing Information Sharing and Analysis Centers (ISACs) from becoming ISAOs, although it is understood that ISAOs encompass a broader need-specific range of activities. The legislative proposal should explain the role of ISACs in the new scheme and positively allow or disallow ISACs from becoming ISAOs. The legislative proposal should also explain the role of other information sharing efforts, such as the Defense Security Information Exchange (DSIE). The new legislation should not bring past successful efforts to a premature end.

Missing from the creation of ISAOs is an explanation of how the "stovepiping effect" prevalent among the ISACs and in other cyber sharing efforts can be eliminated. NIST is working hard to arrive at generally accepted standards for a "cybersecurity framework." Their work should be emulated by having the legislation make clear that the government's role is to learn from industry standards and to conform itself to industry standards rather than the other way around. For example, "best practices" should be specifically recognized as evolving, and industry should have a mechanism to appeal previously determined "best practices." Also, important missing language in the proposed legislation's concept of "information sharing" is that the information sharing should be secure. Otherwise, the value of information sharing is negated.

The proposed legislation's liability protections should include an explicit extension of the Support Anti-Terrorism by Fostering Effective Technologies (SAFETY) Act. Your Committee previously introduced a bill that extended such liability protection, and a similar protection should be included in this legislation. The legislation should include anti-trust protection for entities that share information. A specific concern within the defense industrial base is that existing regulations already require breach notification and mandatory information sharing. Therefore, the proposed legislation needs to provide, in instances where the government requires the sharing or disclosure of information, extended liability protection to companies that are affected.

Thank you for your attention to this letter. NDJA looks forward to working with your Committee on this and other important matters impacting industry. Please do not hesitate to contact us if you have any questions or need any further comments.

Sincerely,

JIMMY THOMAS,
Director of Legislative Policy.

———

LETTER FROM THE AMERICAN BANKERS ASSOCIATION

MARCH 3, 2015.

The Honorable JOHN RATCLIFFE,
Chairman, Subcommittee on Cybersecurity, Infrastructure Protection, and Security Technologies, Committee on Homeland Security, United States House of Representatives, Washington, DC 20515.

The Honorable CEDRIC L. RICHMOND,
Ranking Member, Subcommittee on Cybersecurity, Infrastructure Protection, and Security Technologies, Committee on Homeland Security, United States House of Representatives, Washington, DC 20515.

DEAR CHAIRMAN RATCLIFFE AND RANKING MEMBER RICHMOND: On behalf of the members of the American Bankers Association (ABA), I respectfully request this letter be included as part of the record for your hearing "Industry Perspectives on the President's Cybersecurity Information-Sharing Proposal."

Recent cyber-attacks underscore the need to help all businesses improve their awareness of threats and enhance their response capabilities. The steps taken by the Administration, through the issuance of the February 13, 2015 executive order promoting private sector Cybersecurity information sharing, will help the business community and government agencies share critical threat information more effectively.

While the recent executive order is an important step towards more effective information sharing, it is widely recognized that Congress must also act to pass legislation to fill important gaps that executive action cannot fill. For instance, legislation is necessary to give businesses legal certainty that they have safe harbor against frivolous lawsuits when voluntarily sharing and receiving threat indicators and countermeasures in real time and taking actions to mitigate cyber attacks.

Legislation also needs to offer protections related to public disclosure, regulatory, and antitrust matters in order to increase the timely exchange of information among public and private entities. ABA also believes that legislation needs to safeguard privacy and civil liberties and establish appropriate roles for civilian and intelligence agencies. The financial sector is dedicated to protecting customer data, and has led the way for effective information sharing through the development of the Financial Services Information Sharing and Analysis Center (FS–ISAC). We are committed to working with others within the overall business community to develop a similarly strong and effective mechanism for sharing threat information.

We share the views of the Financial Services Sector Coordinating Council (FSSCC) and the testimony that will be given by Mr. Greg Garcia. However, we would like to highlight two important areas within the executive order: The acceleration of the DHS security clearance process and the establishment of Information Sharing and Analysis Organizations (ISAOs).

Information sharing is of critical importance to the financial services sector, other critical infrastructure sectors and the government. Without it, none of the financial sector's security and resiliency priorities would be achievable. With key federal support from the Treasury Department as our Sector Specific Agency, law enforcement and DHS, our network defenders are better able to prepare for cyber threats when there is a consistent, reliable and sustainable flow of actionable Cybersecurity information and analysis, at both a classified and unclassified level.

As a nation, we are making some progress toward this goal, but it has become increasingly necessary for appropriately-cleared representatives of critical sectors such as financial services to have access, and provide contributions, to classified information that enables analysts and operators to take timely action to defend essential systems. Accordingly, the executive order's enhancement of DHS's role in accelerating the security clearance process for critical sector owners and operators is a clear indication of the Administration's support for this public-private partnership.

The ISAC's have played an important role for critical infrastructure protection information sharing and incident response for their sectors. The FS–ISAC, in particular, enjoys strong support from sector members, Treasury and DHS. In this spirit, we also support the creation of ISAOs as a mechanism for all sectors, regions and other stakeholder groups to share Cybersecurity information and coordinate analysis and response. While ISACs must retain their status as the government's primary critical infrastructure partners, given their mandate for broad sectorial representation, the development of ISAOs should be facilitated for stakeholder groups that require a collaborative cyber and physical threat information sharing capability that builds on the strong foundation laid by the ISACs.

As the ISAO standards development process unfolds, certain principles must be upheld for structuring both the ISAOs themselves and the government's interaction with them:

- Sharing of sensitive security information within and among communities of trust is successful when operational standards of practice establish clear and enforced information handling rules;
- Information sharing is not a competitive sport: while competition in innovation can improve technical capabilities, operational standards should incentivize federated information sharing. Threat and vulnerability intelligence needs to be fused across trust communities, not diffused or siloed;
- Government internal processes for collecting, analyzing and packaging critical infrastructure protection intelligence for ISAC/ISAO consumption must be streamlined and transparent to maximize timeliness, accuracy and relevance of actionable shared information; and
- To manage scarce resources, government information sharing mechanisms such as the National Cyber and Communications Integration Center (NCCIC) and the Treasury Department's Cyber Intelligence Group (CIG) should prioritize engagements with ISACs and ISAOs according to transparently established criteria.

It is also important that the process to develop the ISAO standards is collaborative, open, and transparent. The process managed by the National Institute of Standards and Technology (NIST) during the development of the NIST Cybersecurity Framework is an excellent example of the appropriate leveraging of private sector input, knowledge and experience to develop guidance that will primarily impact non-governmental entities. We encourage DHS, as the implementing authority of the president's EO, to emulate the engagement model that NIST used to create and adopt their Cybersecurity Framework. The process worked.

Finally, for DHS to be successful implementing the EO and its many cyber security risk management and partnership authorities, it must be sufficiently resourced with the best analytical and technical capabilities, with a cadre of highly qualified Cybersecurity leaders and analytical teams to conduct its mission. There must be a concerted effort to recruit, retain and maintain a world class workforce that is able to assess cyber threats globally and help the private sector reduce risk to this nation. With the application of the principles discussed in this statement, we believe the creation of ISAOs and their partnership agreements with DHS have the potential to complement the ISAC foundation and measurably improve cyber risk reduction for critical infrastructure and the national economy.

We look forward to working with Congress, the Administration and DHS to leverage the FS–ISAC as a successful model in the development of regional information sharing and analysis organizations. Above all, we urge Congress to send a bill to the president that gives businesses the liability and antitrust protections, and our citizens the privacy and civil liberty protections that will enhance our already significant efforts to protect the Cybersecurity of our nation.

Although it was not the focal point of the hearing, we understand that an issue may be raised about whether or not requiring PINs on transactions would be a more effective way to prevent harm to consumers. There are some very positive features of PIN transactions, but the fact is that the recent data breaches show the limitations of PINs as a security feature. The recent breaches demonstrate the danger of PINs with debit cards that are directly linked to a person's bank account (e.g., through an ATM). It is possible that if a PIN is stolen from a retailer's system, a criminal could access the customer's entire account and commit fraud.

Security reporter Brian Krebs wrote that there are recent examples, such as with the recent Home Depot breach, of thieves acquiring PINs, changing them, and withdrawing cash from customers' accounts.[1] The data also shows that hackers increasingly target PINs. A report by the Federal Reserve Bank of Atlanta published in 2012 found that PIN debit fraud rates have increased more than threefold since 2004.[2]

The security threat we face now is a complex problem that cannot be solved by any single technology, standard, mandate or regulation. In fact, it cannot be solved by a single sector of society—businesses, standards-setting bodies, policymakers, and law enforcement—must work together to protect the financial and privacy interests of consumers. The attached white paper "Preventing Data Breaches: Smart Security in a Changing Threat Landscape" which was prepared by the ABA, goes into this issue in greater detail. It makes it clear that winning the war against criminal hackers will take a forward-looking approach and the best technologies. No single security feature is fail-proof and including a technology mandate in data breach legislation will only provide a false sense of security and not real protection for consumers.

Sincerely,

JAMES C. BALLENTINE

ATTACHMENT.—PREVENTING DATA BREACHES: SMART SECURITY IN A CHANGING THREAT LANDSCAPE

DYNAMIC CYBERSECURITY FOR THE FUTURE

Recent high-profile data breaches at retailers like Target and Home Depot underscore the critical need for stronger and more innovative security solutions that protect consumers.

Dynamic solutions, not rigid one-size-fits-all mandates. Mandates stifle innovation in the private sector and hinder the ability to adapt and react to evolving threats. While the federal government may believe technology mandates are a way to ensure a level of security, the private sector—and more importantly, consumers—will be saddled with static technology that ultimately makes them vulnerable.

Investing in security. Banks and payment networks continue to invest heavily in the development and implementation of promising new technologies capable of protecting consumers everywhere purchases are made.

A common enemy. Both banks and retailers have a role to play in fighting criminal hackers who will never stop looking for new ways to steal consumers' data.

CHIP TECHNOLOGY: WHY IT WORKS

Debit and credit cards with EMV (Europay MasterCard Visa) or "chip" technology have a microprocessor that protects your personal information through encryption—a process that scrambles personal and financial data to make it virtually useless to criminals. Whether the consumer signs for a purchase or enters a PIN, it is the chip technology that enables a more secure payment. Chip technology cards are:

More secure than magnetic stripe cards, because the chip generates unique data for each transaction. If that information is stolen, it won't be traceable back to the account.

Nearly impossible to replicate, thanks to the chip's ability to create a new, random number for each transaction.

---

[1] http://krebsonsecurity.com/2014/09/in-wake-of-confirmed-breach-at-home-depot-banks-see-spike-in-pin-debit-card-fraud/.
[2] Federal Reserve Bank of Atlanta (2012) http://bit.ly/16RAPGW.

Coming to a checkout terminal near you. Banks are already issuing chip cards, with 120 million cards expected to be in the hands of U.S. consumers by the end of 2014, and 575 million cards issued by the end of 2015. Javelin Strategy and Research estimates only 10 percent of merchants currently have terminals that accept EMV chips. By October 2015, banks must issue cards with chip capability and retailers must have terminals to accept them or they will be liable for fraudulent purchases made on the card.

IT'S THE CHIP THAT MATTERS

For cards with EMV chip technology, it's the chip that makes the card more secure.

A mandate, such as one requiring chip-enabled cards or PINs, does not prevent on-line or mobile fraud. Americans spent $263 billion on-line last year (most often without a PIN) and that dollar number is expected to grow to $414 billion by 2018. Less than 30 percent of merchants in the U.S.—both on-line and traditional storefronts—are currently equipped to accept a PIN: And some merchants prefer not to. As mobile technologies emerge, device passcodes and thumbprints are being introduced to benefit the consumer. Security should be dynamic, useful and address the realities of an increasingly digital economy, not be mandated to a single method.

A mandate could not have prevented the massive data breaches at Target, caused by hackers using malware to steal credentials through the company's heating, ventilating, and air conditioning (HVAC) contractor. It also would not have prevented breaches at Home Depot, and Neiman Marcus, caused by malware installed in checkout terminals. However, chip cards would have reduced the value of the compromised data by inhibiting the creation of counterfeit cards.

Criminals will always seek the weakest link. No single security feature is fail-proof. Creating a mandate around one static technology gives hackers an open invitation to exploit loopholes in the payments system.

No technology is fail-proof. Magnetic stripes have become more vulnerable over the years as criminals have found ways to skim the data stored in the stripe and replicate it to make fraudulent purchases. PINs have their own flaws. A report by the Federal Reserve Bank of Atlanta published in 2012 found that PIN debit fraud rates have increased more than threefold since 2004. When a PIN is compromised, it can open a backdoor for criminals to access and drain consumers' bank accounts at an ATM.

BEYOND PLASTIC: BETTER SECURITY, WHEREVER PURCHASES ARE MADE

EMV chip technology will help protect customers at the register, but it's not a silver bullet. Expecting a single technology to successfully prevent all fraud is unrealistic, which is why banks and payment networks are implementing new technologies that can adapt and deploy in a changing threat landscape:

End-to-end encryption is helping make payments more secure, by encoding consumers' information into unreadable formats as it makes its way from checkout to card network to the bank and back.

Tokenization technology replaces sensitive consumer account information at the cash register or on-line with a random "token," rendering the information useless to criminals. This technology is an important feature for some mobile wallets, such as Apple Pay, and can be used on-line.

24/7 fraud protection is already a hallmark of banks, which employ teams of experts using advanced computer systems to monitor transactions and detect unusual activity indicating a customer's account has been hacked.

THE BOTTOM LINE: FEWER MANDATES, MORE COLLABORATION

Mandates hurt consumers because they funnel valuable time and resources into static technologies that will become obsolete as cyber threats change.

A mandate could drive up the cost of doing business without addressing the fundamental cause of most future data breaches—inconsistent and outdated security practices within the retailers, which was the source of recent high-profile breaches at Target, Home Depot, and others.

The security threat facing the payment card industry is a complex problem that cannot be solved by any single technology, standard, mandate, or regulation. It cannot be solved by a single sector of society—businesses, standards-setting bodies, policymakers, and law enforcement—must work together to protect the financial and privacy interests of consumers.

To borrow a concept from Moore's Law of Innovation, every new technology is obsolete within 18 months. Data security technologies are no exception. Winning the war against cybercrime will take a forward-looking approach to preventing data breaches anywhere they occur—at the register, with a mobile phone or on-line. Money and resources should flow to the best technologies to fight these cyber attacks. Focusing on just one technology gives a false sense of security at a cost that everyone bears.

LETTER FROM THE RETAIL INDUSTRY LEADERS ASSOCIATION

FEBRUARY 25, 2015.

The Honorable MICHAEL MCCAUL,
Chairman, House Committee on Homeland Security, United States House of Representatives, Washington, DC 20515.
The Honorable BENNIE THOMPSON,
Ranking Member, House Committee on Homeland Security, United States House of Representatives, Washington, DC 20515.

DEAR CHAIRMAN MCCAUL AND RANKING MEMBER THOMPSON: On behalf of the Retail Industry Leaders Association (RILA), I write to thank you for holding today's hearing entitled, "Examining the President's Cybersecurity Information-Sharing Proposal." Retailers greatly appreciate the Committee's leadership in seeking to find a sensible path to address critical cybersecurity issues.

RILA is the trade association of the world's largest and most innovative retail companies. RILA members include more than 200 retailers, product manufacturers, and service suppliers, which together are responsible for more than $1.5 trillion in annual sales, millions of American jobs and more than 100,000 stores, manufacturing facilities and distribution centers domestically and abroad.

Retailers embrace innovative technology to provide American consumers with unparalleled services and products on-line, through mobile applications, and in our stores. While technology presents great opportunity, nation states, criminal organizations, and other bad actors also are using it to attack businesses, institutions, and governments. As we have seen, no organization is immune from attacks and no security system is invulnerable. Retailers understand that defense against cyber attacks must be an on-going effort, evolving to address the changing nature of the threat. RILA is committed to working with Congress to give government and retailers the tools necessary to thwart this unprecedented attack on the United States (U.S.) economy and bring the fight to cyber criminals around the globe.

As leaders in the retail community, we are taking new and significant steps to enhance cybersecurity throughout the industry. To that end, RILA formed the Retail Cyber Intelligence Sharing Center (R–CISC), one component of which is a Retail ISAC, in 2014 in partnership with America's most recognized retailers. The Center has opened a steady flow of information sharing between retailers, law enforcement and other relevant stakeholders. These efforts already have helped prevent data breaches, protected millions of American customers and saved retailers millions of dollars. The R–CISC is open to all retailers regardless of their membership in RILA.

For years, RILA members have been developing and deploying new technologies to achieve pioneering levels of security and service. The cyber-attacks that our industry faces change every day and our members are building layered and resilient systems to meet these threats. Key to this effort is the ability to design systems to meet actual threats rather than potentially outdated cybersecurity standards that may be enshrined in law. That is why development of any technical cybersecurity standards, beyond a mandate for reasonable security, must be voluntary and industry-led such as the standards embodied in the National Institute of Standards and Technology Cybersecurity Framework. RILA members using the Framework have found it to be a helpful tool in evaluating their cybersecurity posture and support the continued use of voluntary, industry-led processes as a key method of addressing dynamic technology challenges.

One area of cybersecurity that needs immediate attention is payment card technology. RILA members have long supported the adoption of stronger debit and credit card security protections. The woefully outdated magnetic stripe technology used on cards today is the chief vulnerability in the payments ecosystem. This 1960s-era technology allows cyber criminals to create counterfeit cards and commit fraud with ease. Retailers continue to press banks and card networks to provide U.S. consumers with the same Chip and PIN technology that has proven to dramatically reduce fraud when it has been deployed elsewhere around the world. According to the

Federal Reserve, PINs on debit cards make them 700 percent more secure than transactions authorized by signature.[1]

Increasing cyber threat information sharing is also vital to defeating sophisticated and coordinated cyber actors. RILA strongly supports cybersecurity information sharing legislation that provides liability protections for participating organizations. That liability protection should protect companies that share with appropriate federal law enforcement partners like the Secret Service and the FBI to help bring cybercriminals to justice. Legislation also should increase funding for government-sponsored research into next generation security controls and enhance law enforcement capabilities to investigate and prosecute criminals internationally. The cyber-attacks faced by every sector of our economy constitute a grave national security threat that should be addressed from all angles.

RILA thanks the Committee for holding this important hearing examining cyber information sharing legislation and cybersecurity more broadly. We look forward to working with you on these vital issues. Should you have any additional questions regarding this matter, please feel free to contact Nicholas Ahrens, Vice President, Privacy and Cybersecurity.

Sincerely,

JENNIFER M. SAFAVIAN,
Executive Vice President, Government Affairs.

STATEMENT OF THE FINANCIAL SERVICES INFORMATION SHARING & ANALYSIS CENTER AND THE NATIONAL COUNCIL OF INFORMATION SHARING AND ANALYSIS CENTERS

MARCH 4, 2015

FS–ISAC BACKGROUND

Chairman Ratcliffe and Members of the subcommittee, my name is Denise Anderson. I am vice president, FS–ISAC, government and cross sector programs at the Financial Services Information Sharing & Analysis Center (FS–ISAC) and chair of the National Council of ISACs (NCI). I want to thank you for this opportunity to address the Cybersecurity, Infrastructure Protection and Security Technologies Subcommittee about the industry perspective on "Cybersecurity and Information Sharing". I am submitting this testimony for the record as I am on travel and regret my inability to take part in this proceeding.

The FS–ISAC was formed in 1999 in response to the 1998 Presidential Decision Directive 63 (PDD 63), which called for the public and private sectors to work together to address cyber threats to the Nation's critical infrastructures. After 9/11, in response to Homeland Security Presidential Directive 7 (its 2013 successor, Presidential Policy Directive 21) and the Homeland Security Act, the FS–ISAC expanded its role to encompass physical threats to the sector.

The FS–ISAC is a 501(c)6 nonprofit organization and is funded entirely by its member firms and sponsors. In 2004, there were only 68 members of the FS–ISAC, mostly larger financial services firms. Since that time the membership has expanded to almost 5,500 organizations including commercial banks and credit unions of all sizes, markets and equities firms, brokerage firms, insurance companies, payments processors, and 24 trade associations representing virtually all of the U.S. financial services sector. The FS–ISAC is a global organization and has members in 38 different countries.

NCI BACKGROUND

The NCI is a voluntary organization of ISACs formed in 2003 in recognition of the need for the ISACs to share information with each other about common threats and issues. The mission of the NCI is to advance the physical and cyber security of the critical infrastructure of North America by establishing and maintaining a framework for valuable interaction among and between the ISACs and with Government. The membership of the NCI is the 18 individual ISACs that represent their respective sectors or sub-sectors. The NCI also works closely with the other critical infrastructure sectors (CI) that have operational arms including chemical, (reforming its ISAC) automotive (currently forming an ISAC) and critical manufacturing, among others. The NCI has made it a goal to be inclusive of each critical infrastructure sector and sub-sector's operational arm.

---

[1] Federal Reserve, "2011 Interchange Fee Revenue, Covers Issuer Costs, and Covered Issuer and Merchant Fraud Losses Related to Debit Card Transactions," (March 5, 2013).

The ISACs collaborate with each other daily through the NCI daily operations centers cyber call, the NCI secure portal and the NCI listserver. The NCI also hosts a weekly operations centers physical call and meets monthly to discuss issues and threats. The organization is a true cross-sector partnership engaged in sharing cyber and physical threats, mitigation strategies and working together and with government partners during incidents requiring cross-sector response as well as addressing issues affecting industry. In addition to the secure portal, the NCI hosts an ISAC threat level dash board, conducts and participates in cross-sector exercises, works with the National Infrastructure Coordinating Center (NICC) and the National Cybersecurity and Communications Integration Center (NCCIC) during steady-state and incidents, holds emergency calls as needed and develops joint white papers around threats. The ISACs have been instrumental in embracing, developing and advancing the automatic exchange of data within their memberships and across the ISACs, as well as with government as possible.

ISACS AND GOVERNMENT PARTNERSHIPS

ISACs, which are not-for-profit organizations, work closely with various Government agencies including their respective Sector Specific Agencies (SSAs) where they exist, intelligence agencies, law enforcement, and State and local governments. In partnership with the Department of Homeland Security (DHS), several ISACs participate in the National Cybersecurity and Communications Integration Center (NCCIC) watch floor. ISAC representatives, cleared at the Top Secret/Sensitive Compartmented Information (TS/SCI) level, attend the daily briefs and other NCCIC meetings to share information on threats, vulnerabilities, incidents, and potential or known impacts to the critical infrastructure sectors. Having ISACs on the floor has allowed for effective collaboration on threats and incidents and there have been many examples of successful information sharing. The ISACs also serve as liaisons to the National Infrastructure Coordinating Center (NICC) and play a vital role in incident response and collaboration under the Critical Infrastructure Partner Annex to the Incident Management Plan.

In addition, ISAC representatives sit on the Cyber Unified Coordination Group (Cyber UCG). This group was set up under authority of the National Cyber Incident Response Plan (NCIRP) and has been actively engaged in incident response.

Finally, it should be noted that the ISACs collaborate with their sector coordinating councils as applicable and work with other critical infrastructure partners during steady state and incidents.

THE FEBRUARY 2015 EXECUTIVE ORDER AND ISAOS

The Executive Order, Promoting Private Sector Cybersecurity Information Sharing, signed February 15, 2013 by President Obama and recently-announced information-sharing legislative proposal are commendable in their intent to foster information sharing. Information Sharing and Analysis Organizations (ISAOs) were first defined in the Homeland Security Act of 2002. ISACs were created under Presidential Decision Directive 63 (PDD–63). Effectively ISACs were the original ISAOs, are the subject-matter experts in information sharing and a majority of ISACs have been in existence for over a decade or more.

Indeed there is a need for many groups that may not fall in with the critical infrastructure sectors such as legal and media and entertainment organizations, who are increasingly becoming targets for cyber incidents and attacks, to share information. The private sector is already organizing efforts in this area and as an example; the FS–ISAC has been working with the legal industry for almost a year now to form an ISAO. Many of the other ISACs, such as the Multi-State ISAC (MS–ISAC) and Information Technology ISAC (IT–ISAC) have also been engaging industries that do not have established information-sharing forums such as the Retail sector, which is actively forming an ISAC.

However ISACs are much more than ISAOs. They serve a special role in critical infrastructure protection and resilience and play a unique role in the sector partnership model. While the White House has noted that the EO seeks to "not limit effective existing relationships that exist between the Government and the private sector" the recent EO and prominent coverage of ISAOs has led to some confusion within industry as to the impacts to ISACs. It is absolutely essential that the successful efforts that the ISACs have established over the years should not be disrupted. It is clear that the ISACs by their success meet the distinct and unique needs of each of their sectors and the owner and operator members of those sectors.

The solution to easing this confusion is very simple. The White House, SSAs—including DHS—and other relevant agencies need to call out, recognize, and support the unique role ISACs play in critical infrastructure protection and resilience. For instance, ISACs have the responsibility to maintain sector-wide threat awareness within their respective sectors. It is critical that our Federal partners continue to respect and support that role to avoid undermining one of the main duties of ISACs to their members and sectors. It is vital that the process is not diluted and remains streamlined to facilitate effective situational awareness and response activities particularly when an incident occurs.

One of the greatest strengths of ISACs is the productive information sharing that occurs by having robust trusted networks of members. Government should support private-sector efforts to form ISACs in those very few critical infrastructure sectors where ISACs do not currently exist, and where they do, regularly and consistently encourage owner/operators to join their respective ISACs. This has been very effective in the financial sector where the United States Department of the Treasury, the regulators, and State agencies have been strongly encouraging membership in the FS–ISAC as a best practice. Currently, not all of the SSAs support their sector-designated ISACs in the same manner.

Attached is an appendix, which lists out some 20 points as to why ISACs are more than ISAOs.

CREATING STANDARDS FOR ISAOS

The Executive Order also calls for the drafting of a set of voluntary standards. The NCI believes that having an established set of capabilities is important and currently has a baseline set of criteria that ISACs must meet in order to be members of the Council. But it is essential that information-sharing organizations have the flexibility and ability to meet the unique needs of its sector and members. Although all ISACs have similar missions, no two ISACs are exactly alike.

Any criteria that are developed must be done in concert with the private sector and must be upheld by the private sector in order to be effective. ISACs and ensuing ISAOs are private-sector organizations. Any attempt by Government to oversee or mandate what these organizations produce and how they collaborate would eliminate information sharing and almost two decades of progress. In the face of growing, targeted and sophisticated threats, rendering proven information-sharing efforts ineffective would not only be a grave consequence, it would run contrary to the spirit of the drafting of the EO: To promote private-sector cybersecurity information sharing.

The NCI has a strong history of mentoring and supporting the establishment of several new ISACs such as Aviation, Retail, and Automotive and the re-formation of the Oil and Gas ISAC. ISACs fostered by activities developed and sponsored by the NCI are robustly sharing among their peer ISACs and partners, items such as best practice guides and toolkits that ISACs can replicate and provide to their members for free.

These activities reflect a powerful force in organizational information sharing and collaboration that the EO fails to contemplate and appears to attempt to recreate through the development of a standards organization. Any focus on ISAOs and ISAO standards must be implemented carefully as not only to encourage and foster information sharing and analytical maturity among newly-established organizations, but also clearly publish, highlight, and fully leverage and emulate aspects of the status quo that are working and have been working for quite some time.

EFFECTIVE INFORMATION SHARING

It is important to note that the goal of information sharing is not to share information in and of itself but to create situational awareness in order to inform risk-based decisions as well as allow operational components within owner/operation organizations that have direct actionable control over the content they are sharing, to perform an action. The focus needs to be on enhancing the ability of operational groups to work closely with each other.

The ISACs are successful organizations with almost two decades of proven cases studies of information sharing and collaboration. They are the subject-matter experts on information sharing. In order for information sharing to be effective it must be:
- Voluntary—not mandated or regulated
- Industry Driven
- Actionable, Timely and Relevant
- Bi-directional and Collaborative

Government can help this effort by:
- Recognizing ISACs and the special operational role that they play in critical infrastructure protection and resilience;

- Supporting private-sector efforts to form ISACs in the very few critical infra-structure sectors where they do not currently exist;
- Encourage owners and operators of critical infrastructure to join their respective sector ISACs;
- Facilitate getting all of the ISACs on the NCCIC floor. After 4 years this still has not been accomplished;
- Recognize the NCI as the coordinating body for the ISACs.

This concludes my written statement for the record. Thank you again for the opportunity to present this testimony and I look forward to your questions.

APPENDIX: 20 REASONS WHY ISACS ARE MORE THAN ISAOS

- ISACs are all-hazards and address both cyber and physical threats and incidents
- ISACs are the designated operational arms of their sectors
- ISACs play a critical industry- and Government-recognized role in critical infra-structure incident response
- ISACs have reach into their sectors and in many cases are relied upon as the threat and incident communications channel for their respective sectors
- ISACs provide annonymization and aggregation of data for their sectors
- ISACs provide a sector perspective on threats and incidents and provide sector-specific analysis
- ISACs set or manage threat levels for their respective sectors
- ISACs perform structured collaboration across the sectors
- ISACs conduct joint analysis to develop joint products on specific threats and incidents
- ISACs serve an operational role in the National partnership framework
- Many ISACs have security operations centers that monitor threats, vulnerabilities, and incidents and provide analysis for sector threat potential and impact
- ISACs are not-for-profit organizations that are not in the business to sell information but to facilitate it
- ISACs meet the unique needs of their respective members/sectors
- Most ISACs are global and are not just focused on the United States. Many have global partnerships
- ISACs have a vetting process for members to qualify to join
- ISACs are organized and run by the owners and operators of critical infrastructure
- ISACs have a formal governance structure
- ISACS facilitate bi-directional information sharing on incidents, information, and intelligence within and among the sectors.
- ISACs are designated operational entities within sectors to enhance efficiency and coordination of information sharing and incident response.

Mr. RATCLIFFE. The Chairman now recognizes the gentleman from Rhode Island, Mr. Langevin, for an opening statement.

Mr. LANGEVIN. Thank you, Mr. Chairman.

I know that Ranking Member Richmond is on his way, and on his behalf I will just welcome our witnesses.

In particular, I want to acknowledge Greg Garcia, whom I worked with when I chaired this subcommittee many years ago and when you had the Department of Homeland Security.

I thank all of you for your work. I know in one way or another I have had the opportunity to interact with all of our witnesses. Thank you for the work you are doing to better protect our country. I look forward to hearing your perspective here today.

Mr. Chairman, I especially want to commend you for holding this hearing today. Thank you for giving the information-sharing and data breach issues the attention that it needs and deserves. Hearing from expert witnesses I know will move this issue ahead further.

Obviously, there is no one answer to solving our cybersecurity challenges. It is never a problem to be solved, as I have said many times, but it is a problem to be managed, and we have to do a much better job of getting to a place where we are much better protected in cyber space than where we are. We can close that air of vulnerability down to something much more manageable.

It won't be just a Government answer, of course, and it is not going to be just private sector. It is going to take that collaboration of us working together to solve this and deal with this incredible challenge.

So, with that, I will yield back.

I thank our witnesses in advance for being here and what they are about to say.

Thank you, Mr. Chairman. I yield back.

Mr. RATCLIFFE. I thank the gentleman. I remind other Members that additional statements may be submitted for the record.

[The statement of Ranking Member Richmond follows:]

STATEMENT OF RANKING MEMBER CEDRIC L. RICHMOND

MARCH 4, 2015

Our infrastructure is more digitally interconnected than ever. Our country's reliance on cyber systems and networks covers everything from power plants to pipelines, and hospitals to highways. Yet for all the advantages interconnectivity offers, our Nation's critical infrastructure is also increasingly vulnerable to attack from an array of cyber threats.

We are to hear testimony today on how we can be better prepared for these threats. The President has proposed an updated package of legislative initiatives to frame the issues, and hopefully spur Congress to action on cybersecurity. Last year this subcommittee was the author of important authorizations that gave the Department sound footing to carry out its mission as the central civilian portal for information sharing between critical infrastructure sectors and the Government.

It is widely recognized that more is needed, and the President's initiatives do indeed go further. Senator Carper, Ranking Member on the Senate Homeland Security and Government Affairs Committee, has already introduced almost a word-for-word version of the White House information-sharing language as S. 456, The Cyber Threat Sharing Act of 2015.

Hacks on major businesses and financial institutions continue to dominate headlines. Just a few weeks after Anthem insurance announced that account information of as many as 80 million customers had been stolen, we are all waiting for the next shoe to fall.

The President's proposal seeks to create a friendlier atmosphere for companies to swap certain types of computer data with each other and the Government, in order to identify potential cyber threats and isolate security flaws. To persuade companies to buy into the proposed system, the White House bill would provide assurances that the sharing of indicators—which could include things like IP addresses, routing information, and date and time stamps deemed important to identifying potential cyber threats or security vulnerabilities—would be exempt from legal or regulatory punishment. The President's proposals contain some new ideas about the formation of information-sharing organizations that would set sharing standards and privacy requirements.

Since the '90s, firms have shared information directly on an ad hoc basis and through private-sector, nonprofit organizations, such as Information Sharing and Analysis Centers, or ISACs that can analyze and disseminate information. The White House proposal requires the Secretary of Homeland Security to form a new type of organization, the Information Sharing and Analysis Organizations, or ISAOs.

We need to know what kinds of barriers to information sharing exist today, and how we on this subcommittee can help make this cyber tool more effective. For our side, information sharing must be structured in the public and private sectors to ensure that the risks to privacy rights and civil liberties of individual citizens be recognized, and how those rights and liberties can best be protected. Today, hopefully we'll find answers to some of these questions.

We live in a post-Snowden world, and we are all much more aware of the powerful abilities of our surveillance agencies. Information sharing is not a zero-sum game. As policy makers we can step back and take stock of how best to protect our citizen's privacy rights, while finding effective and powerful tools to combat the cyber threats before us.

Mr. RATCLIFFE. We are pleased to have with us a distinguished panel of witnesses today on this very important topic. I would ask all of you to stand, if you would, and raise your right hand.

[Witnesses sworn.]

Mr. RATCLIFFE. Thank you. You may be seated.

Our witnesses today—we have with us Mr. Matthew Eggers. He is the senior director for national security and emergency preparedness at the U.S. Chamber of Commerce.

Mr. Eggers, good to see you again.

Mr. EGGERS. Good to see you.

Mr. RATCLIFFE. Also with us is Ms. Mary Ellen Callahan. She is a partner at Jenner & Block and is the former chief privacy officer at the Department of Homeland Security.

Welcome, Ms. Callahan.

Also with us is Mr. Greg Garcia. He is the executive director of the Financial Services Sector Coordinating Council.

Mr. Garcia, we appreciate you coming to see us today.

Then, finally, last, but not least, Dr. Martin Libicki is the senior management scientist at The RAND Corporation.

Dr. Libicki, thank you for being here as well.

The witnesses' full statements will appear in the record.

The Chairman now recognizes Mr. Eggers for 5 minutes to testify.

STATEMENT OF MATTHEW J. EGGERS, SENIOR DIRECTOR, NATIONAL SECURITY AND EMERGENCY PREPAREDNESS, U.S. CHAMBER OF COMMERCE

Mr. EGGERS. Good afternoon, Chairman Ratcliffe and other distinguished Members of the subcommittee.

My name is Matthew Eggers. I lead the U.S. Chamber Cybersecurity Working Group, which has about 200 members, and it is growing virtually daily. Before talking about the cyber information-sharing proposals, I want to note that my written statement highlights the successful roll-out of the NIST framework.

The Chamber's proudly launched its own cyber campaign under the banner of improving today, protecting tomorrow. In 2014, we organized several roundtables across the country. The events featured State and local chambers and principals from the White House, DHS, NIST, as well as local FBI and Secret Service officials. More roundtables are being planned this year.

The framework would be incomplete without enacting legislation that removes legal and regulatory barriers to quickly exchanging data about threats to U.S. companies. Let's consider CISA and the White House proposal or the Carper bill, S. 456.

First, the draft Cybersecurity Information Sharing Act of 2015, or CISA. In January, 35 associations, including the Chamber, urged the Senate to quickly pass the cyber info-sharing bill modeled after the bipartisan CISA bill that Senators Feinstein and Chambliss championed last year.

The first version of CISA stalled, unfortunately. A draft CISA, 2.0, if you will, sponsored by Senators Burr and Feinstein, is expected to be marked up soon. It reflects practical compromises among many stakeholders. We need to focus our collective legislative negotiations on CISA.

CISA would give businesses legal certainty that they have safe harbor against frivolous lawsuits when voluntarily sharing and receiving cyber threat indicators, or CTIs, and countermeasures in real time with private and public entities and when monitoring information systems to mitigate cyber attacks.

CISA would also offer protections related to public disclosure, (direct) regulatory, and anti-trust matters. Under CISA, businesses must remove personal information from threat indicators before sharing them.

Second, the White House cybersecurity legislative proposal, or S. 456, the Cyber Threat Sharing Act of 2015. Senator Tom Carper introduced S. 456 about 3 weeks ago. I focus, in part, on this bill because it is very similar to the White House's January 13 cyber information-sharing proposal and it has been introduced.

In contrast to CISA, White House/Carper would grant liability protections to companies only when sharing CTIs with DHS's NCCIC and ISAOs, or Information Sharing and Analysis Organizations, that have self-certified that they are following certain information-sharing practices which have not yet been established and won't be for some time.

DHS is to sponsor an outside organization to determine what would constitute cyber info-sharing standards or best practices, even though leading sectors tell us that they already have them. The bottom line: The ISAOs-plus-standards-setting effort warrants scrutiny before our organization supports it.

Also, unlike CISA, businesses would not be protected under White House/Carper when monitoring information systems and sharing and receiving countermeasures. The White House/Carper bill would not write anti-trust protections into the Federal law.

The lack of safeguards and protections in all of these areas would deter industry from participating in these information-sharing programs for fear of litigation or liability, whether at the Federal or the State levels.

CISA and White House/Carper do share some common features especially in the area of privacy and civil liberties protection. Both CISA and the White House/Carper proposal narrowly define what cyber threat indicators may be shared among private and Government entities.

CISA and White House/Carper require that businesses remove personal information from CTIs before sharing them. Like CISA, the White House/Carper bill would tightly limit how the Federal Government could use threat indicators that agencies receive.

In sum, when comparing CISA with White House/Carper, CISA offers a more dynamic way to share cyber threat data among many businesses and Government entities, coupled with strong liability and related protections.

CISA would go the furthest in helping businesses, including critical infrastructure, defend information systems against cyber attacks while protecting privacy.

CISA is meant to help counter serious malicious attacks aimed at America that are being launched from threats like organized crime and state-sponsored groups.

Getting an information-sharing bill signed into law this year, one that would actually incentivize industry to participate, not back away, is the Chamber's top cyber legislative priority.

Again, thank you for inviting me to be here today. I would be happy to answer any questions. Thank you.

[The prepared statement of Mr. Eggers follows:]

PREPARED STATEMENT OF MATTHEW J. EGGERS

MARCH 4, 2015

Good morning, Chairman Ratcliffe, Ranking Member Richmond, and other distinguished Members of the committee. My name is Matthew Eggers, and I am a senior director of the U.S. Chamber's National Security and Emergency Preparedness Department. On behalf of the Chamber, I welcome the opportunity to testify before the Subcommittee on Cybersecurity, Infrastructure Protection, and Security Technologies regarding industry's perspectives on the President's cybersecurity information-sharing proposal.

The Chamber's National Security and Emergency Preparedness Department was established in 2003 to develop and implement the Chamber's homeland and National security policies. The department works through the National Security Task Force, a policy committee composed of roughly 200 Chamber members representing practically every sector of the American economy. The task force's Cybersecurity Working Group, which I lead, identifies current and emerging issues, crafts policies and positions, and provides analysis and direct advocacy to Government and business leaders. Industry's interest in cybersecurity is healthy and expanding—individuals join the working group almost daily.

The need to address increasingly sophisticated threats against U.S. and global businesses has gone from an IT issue to a top priority for the C-suite and the boardroom. Chamber President and CEO Thomas J. Donohue recently said, "In an interconnected world, economic security and national security are linked. To maintain a strong and resilient economy, we must protect against the threat of cyberattacks."

My statement highlights the successful rollout of the National Institute of Standards and Technology's (NIST's) *Framework for Improving Critical Infrastructure Cybersecurity* (the framework)[1] and the positive collaboration that many businesses and Government entities have developed over the past several months, including the Chamber's cybersecurity campaign—*Improving Today. Protecting Tomorrow*™.

I am also going to focus on policy issues—information-sharing legislation being the top legislative priority—that lawmakers and the administration need to diligently address. The information-sharing discussion puts too little emphasis on improving Government-to-business sharing. The Chamber wants to expand Government-to-business information sharing, which is progressing but needs improvement.[2]

The framework is a good start, but more work is needed to push back against skilled attackers. Most small and mid-size businesses (SMBs) tend to lack the money and personnel to beat back highly-advanced and nefarious actors, such as organized criminal gangs and groups carrying out state-sponsored attacks. No single strategy can prevent advanced and persistent threats—popularly known as APTs in cybersecurity jargon—from breaching an organization's cyber defenses.

Policymakers have not sufficiently acknowledged this expensive, practical reality. American companies should not be expected to shoulder the substantial costs of cyber attacks emanating from well-resourced bad actors such as criminal syndicates or nation-states—costs typically absorbed by national governments. Nation-states or their proxies and other sophisticated actors are apparently hacking businesses with impunity—and that has got to stop.

In addition to having policymakers acknowledge cost concerns, the Chamber would welcome working with the administration and Congress on establishing an intelligent and forceful deterrence strategy, utilizing an array of U.S. policy tools,

---

[1] See *www.nist.gov/cyberframework*.

[2] The Chamber submitted in October 2014 similar comments to the National Institute of Standards and Technology (NIST) related to businesses' awareness and use of the framework. See *http://csrc.nist.gov/cyberframework/rfi_comments_10_2014.html*.

which the United States currently lacks. U.S. policymakers need to focus on pushing back against illicit actors and not on blaming the victims of cybersecurity incidents.[3]

THE FRAMEWORK IS AN EXCELLENT EXAMPLE OF AN EFFECTIVE PUBLIC-PRIVATE PART-NERSHIP. CRITICAL INFRASTRUCTURE AWARENESS OF THE FRAMEWORK IS STRONG, AND SECTOR ACTIVITIES ARE ROBUST AND MATURING

The Chamber believes that the framework—which was released last February—has been a success. The framework represents one of the best examples of public-private partnerships in action. NIST and stakeholders in the public and private sectors should have a great sense of accomplishment. The Chamber, sector-based coordinating councils and associations, companies, and other entities collaborated closely with NIST in developing the framework since the first workshop was held in April 2013.

Critical infrastructure sectors are keenly aware of and supportive of the framework. The Chamber understands that critical infrastructures at "greatest risk" have been identified and engaged by administration officials under the terms of the cyber executive order (EO).[4] Government officials ought to ensure that all resources, particularly the latest cyber threat indicators (CTIs), are available to these enterprises to counter increasing and advanced threats.

Further, important elements of U.S. industry are aware of the framework and are using it or similar risk management tools. Indeed, the Chamber welcomed an assessment from Michael Daniel, White House special assistant to the President and cybersecurity coordinator, who remarked on September 23, 2014, at the Chamber's third cyber roundtable in Everett, Washington, that industry's response to the framework has been "phenomenal."

A second White House official, Ari Schwartz, senior director for cybersecurity, noted on October 1, 2014, that business support for the framework has "exceeded expectations." Such recognition is constructive and helps keep the private sector engaged in using the framework and promoting it with business partners.[5]

Much of industry's favorable reaction is owed in large measure to NIST, which tackled the framework's development in ways that ought to serve as a model for other agencies and departments. In May 2014, the administration sent the business community a powerful message, saying that the framework should remain collaborative, voluntary, and innovative over the long term.[6] Interestingly, public focus on the framework has created visibility into industry's long-standing efforts to address cyber risks and threats—constant, dedicated, and mostly silent efforts that preceded the creation of the framework.[7]

Most notable, since the framework's release, industry has demonstrated its commitment to using it. Many associations are creating resources for their members and holding events across the country and taking other initiatives to promote cybersecurity education and awareness of the framework. Some examples are listed here. Associations are planning and exploring additional activities as well.

- The Alliance of Automobile Manufacturers and the Association of Global Automakers have initiated a process to establish an automobile industry sector information-sharing and analysis center (Auto–ISAC) to voluntarily collect and share information about existing or potential threats to the cybersecurity of motor vehicle electronics and in-vehicle networks.
- The American Chemistry Council (ACC) is developing sector-specific guidance based on the NIST cyber framework to further enhance and implement the

---

[3] The Chamber submitted comments to the Department of Homeland Security (DHS) on cybersecurity solutions for small and mid-size businesses (SMBs) in April 2014.

[4] Executive Order (EO) 13636, *Improving Critical Infrastructure Cybersecurity,* is available at *www.gpo.gov/fdsys/pkg/FR-2013-02-19/pdf/2013-03915.pdf.*

[5] See "At eight-month mark, industry praises framework and eyes next steps," *Inside Cybersecurity,* October 6, 2014, *http://insidecybersecurity.com/Cyber-Daily-News/Daily-News/at-eight-month-mark-industry-praises-framework-and-eyes-next-steps/menu-id-1075.html.*

[6] The Chamber agrees with Michael Daniel's May 22 blog, *Assessing Cybersecurity Regulations,* at *www.whitehouse.gov/blog/2014/05/22/assessing-cybersecurity-regulations.* The blog says that business and Government "must build equally agile and responsive capabilities not bound by outdated and inflexible rules and procedures." The Chamber and industry partners especially urge independent agencies and Congress to adhere to the dynamic approach advocated by the administration and embodied in the nonregulatory, public-private framework. See June 11, 2014, multiassociation letter, which is available at *www.uschamber.com/sites/default/files/documents/files/11June14GroupLetterT-YReplytoDanielCyberBlog_Final_0.pdf.*

[7] The on-line publication *Inside Cybersecurity* provides an excellent catalog of industry initiatives to implement data- and network-security best practices. See *http://insidecybersecurity.com/Sectors/menu-id-1149.html.*

council's Responsible Care® Security Code. ACC's Chemical Information Technology Center (ChemITC) is also piloting an ISAC for the chemical sector.

- The American Gas Association (AGA) has hosted a series of webinars on control system cybersecurity, is collaborating with small utilities to develop robust cybersecurity programs, and is working with companies to review and enhance their cybersecurity posture using the Oil and Natural Gas Subsector Cybersecurity Capability Maturity Model (ONG–C2M2) from the Department of Energy (DOE). Among other activities, AGA has stood up the Downstream Natural Gas Information and Analysis Center (DNG–ISAC), an ISAC designed to help support the information-sharing interests of downstream natural gas utilities.
- The American Hotel & Lodging Association (AH&LA) has conducted a series of widely-attended cyber and data security webinars to assist small, medium, and large hotel and lodging businesses with implementing key information security measures and risk assessments.
- The American Water Works Association (AWWA) has created cybersecurity guidance and a use-case tool to aid water and wastewater utilities' implementation of the framework. The guidance is cross-referenced to the framework. This tool serves as implementation guidance for the framework in the water and wastewater systems sector.
- Members of the Communications Sector Coordinating Council (CSCC)—made up of broadcasting, cable, wireline, wireless, and satellite segments—have participated in multiple NIST, Department of Homeland Security (DHS), and industry association-sponsored programs, webinars, and panels. The sector is completing a year-long effort within the Federal Communication Commission's (FCC's) Communications Security Reliability and Interoperability Council (CSRIC), which involves more than 100 professionals who have worked to adapt the NIST framework to the sector segments and provide guidance to the industry.
- The Electricity Subsector Coordinating Council has worked with DOE to develop sector-specific guidance for using the framework. The guidance leverages existing subsector-specific approaches to cybersecurity, including DOE's *Electricity Subsector Cybersecurity Risk Management Process Guideline*, the *Electricity Subsector Cybersecurity Capability Maturity Model*, NIST's *Guidelines for Smart Grid Cyber Security*, and the North American Electric Reliability Corporation's (NERC's) Critical Infrastructure Protection Cybersecurity Standards.
- The mutual fund industry, represented by the Investment Company Institute (ICI), has added to its committee roster a Chief Information Security Officer Advisory Committee. The committee's mission is to collaborate on cybersecurity issues and information sharing in the financial services industry and provide a cyber threat protection resource for ICI members.
- The Information Technology Industry Council (ITI) visited Korea and Japan in May 2014 and shared with these countries' governments and business leaders the benefits of a public-private partnership-based approach to developing globally workable cybersecurity policies. ITI highlighted the framework as an example of an effective policy developed in this manner, reflecting global standards and industry-driven practices. ITI principals also spoke at a U.S.-European Union (EU) workshop in Brussels in November 2014, comparing U.S. and E.U. policy approaches with cybersecurity and emphasizing the positive attributes of the framework and its development.
- The National Association of Manufacturers (NAM) has spearheaded the D.A.T.A. (Driving the Agenda for Technology Advancement) Policy Center, providing manufacturers with a forum to understand the latest cybersecurity policy trends, threats, and best practices. The D.A.T.A. Center focuses on working with small and medium-size manufacturers to help them secure their assets.
- Through the American Petroleum Institute (API), the oil and natural gas sector has worked with DOE to complete the Oil and Natural Gas Subsector Cybersecurity Capability Maturity Model (ONG–C2M2). The oil and natural gas sector in 2014 established an Oil and Natural Gas Information Sharing and Analysis Center (ONG–ISAC) to provide shared intelligence on cyber incidents, threats, vulnerabilities, and responses throughout the industry.
- The Retail Industry Leaders Association (RILA), in partnership with the National Retail Federation (NRF), created the Retail Cyber Intelligence Sharing Center (R–CISC), featuring information sharing, research, and education and training. This ISAC enables retailers to share threat data among themselves and to receive threat information from Government and law enforcement partners.

- The U.S. Chamber of Commerce has launched its National roundtable series, *Improving Today. Protecting Tomorrow*™, recommending that businesses of all sizes and sectors adopt fundamental internet security practices.

POLICYMAKERS NEED TO FOCUS ON PASSING INFORMATION-SHARING LEGISLATION AND DETERRING FOREIGN ATTACKERS. THE CHAMBER'S CYBERSECURITY CAMPAIGN ENTERS ITS SECOND YEAR

The NIST framework is designed to help start a cybersecurity program or improve an existing one. The framework puts cybersecurity into a common language for organizations to better understand their cybersecurity posture, set goals for cybersecurity improvements, monitor their progress, and foster communications with internal and external stakeholders. Looking ahead to 2015, the Chamber's cybersecurity campaign intends to focus on several areas, including the following:

Improving information sharing is job No. 1. The framework would be incomplete without enacting information-sharing legislation that removes legal and regulatory barriers to quickly exchanging data about threats to U.S. companies.

- *Draft Cybersecurity Information Sharing Act (CISA) of 2015.*—On January 27, 35 associations, including the Chamber, urged the Senate to quickly pass a cybersecurity information-sharing bill.[8] The Senate Intelligence Committee passed in July 2014 S. 2588, the Cybersecurity Information Sharing Act (CISA) of 2014, a smart and workable bill, which earned broad bipartisan support.

  The committee released in February a new draft bill—CISA 2015—for stakeholder review. Recent cyber incidents underscore the need for legislation to help businesses improve their awareness of cyber threats and enhance their protection and response capabilities.

  The Chamber urges Congress to send a bill to the President that gives businesses legal certainty that they have safe harbor against frivolous lawsuits when voluntarily sharing and receiving threat indicators and countermeasures in real time with multiple private and public entities, as well as when monitoring information systems to mitigate cyberattacks.

  The legislation also needs to offer protections related to public disclosure, regulatory, and anti-trust matters in order to increase the timely exchange of technical CTIs and countermeasures among public and private entities.

  The Chamber further believes that legislation needs to safeguard privacy and civil liberties and establish appropriate roles for civilian and intelligence agencies. For example, businesses must remove personal information from CTIs before sharing them. Private entities must share "electronic mail or media, an interactive form on an internet website, or a real time, automated process between information systems" with DHS—a civilian entity—if they are to be offered protection from liability.

  CISA, which is sponsored by Sens. Richard Burr and Dianne Feinstein, reflects practical compromises among many stakeholders on these issues. At the time of this writing, the measure is expected to be marked up the week of March 9. The Chamber looks forward to reviewing the bill following the mark-up to determine its support for the base measure and any amendments. Industry is likely to strongly support CISA.

- *White House cybersecurity legislative proposal (S. 456, the Cyber Threat Sharing Act of 2015).*—On February 11, S. 456, the Cyber Threat Sharing Act of 2015, was introduced in the Senate by Sen. Tom Carper. It makes sense to refer to S. 456 because it is very similar to the White House's cybersecurity information-sharing proposal, which was discussed at last week's House Homeland Security Committee hearing, and released by the administration on January 13.[9]

  CISA offers strong protections and flexible avenues for sharing with public and private entities. In contrast, S. 456 would grant liability protections to companies only when sharing CTIs with (1) DHS' National Cybersecurity and Communications Integration Center (NCCIC)—excluding law enforcement agencies, among others—or with (2) information-sharing and analysis organizations (ISAOs) that have self-certified that they are following information-sharing best practices. (The implications of the ISAOs and the new White House executive order [10] related to promoting cybersecurity information sharing, which directs DHS to sponsor an ISAO standards organization to establish a common set of

[8] The coalition letter is available at *www.uschamber.com/sites/default/files/150127_multi-association_cyber_info-sharing_legislation_senate.pdf.*
[9] *http://homeland.house.gov/hearing/hearing-administration-s-cybersecurity-legislative-proposal-information-sharing; www.whitehouse.gov/omb/legislative_letters* (see January 13, 2015).
[10] *www.whitehouse.gov/the-press-office/2015/02/13/executive-order-promoting-private-sector-cybersecurity-information-shari.*

voluntary standards for creating and operating ISAOs, have not been fully assessed by industry.)

These two protected avenues for sharing CTIs are far too narrow and limiting and do not reflect the information-sharing relationships that businesses have built up over time, for instance, with DHS, the Departments of Energy and Treasury, and law enforcement agencies.

Unlike CISA, businesses would not be protected under S. 456 when monitoring information systems and sharing or receiving countermeasures. The lack of safeguards in these areas is a fundamental weakness of the White House proposal and S. 456.

Under S. 456, cyber threat data shared with the NCCIC would seemingly be protected from public disclosure and may not be used as evidence in a regulatory action against the entity that shared CTIs, which is welcome. However, S. 456 neither codifies antitrust protections in Federal law nor preempts State law. The bill simply references via a sense-of-Congress provision a policy statement that was issued in April 2014 by the Department of Justice and the Federal Trade Commission.[11] While this provision is constructive, anti-trust protections need to be written into law to be meaningful to industry.

Similar to CISA, S. 456 includes strong privacy protections. Both bills *narrowly define what CTIs may be shared* among private sector and Federal Government entities.[12] CISA and S. 456 require that businesses *remove personal information from CTIs* before sharing them. The Chamber urges businesses to share cybersecurity threat data with industry partners and the Government. Still, the mandate to scrub personal information would almost certainly sideline smaller businesses, because the provision assumes that businesses would have the technical know-how or the resources to scrub data. To be sure, this outcome is not the intent of the bills' writers, but it is important to note that this is the likely response many businesses would have to such provisions.

And, like CISA, S. 456 would also tightly limit how the Federal Government could use CTIs that agencies receive. However, unlike CISA, S. 456 would sunset after 5 years. A sunset provision would almost certainly inhibit businesses' ability to make long-term planning decisions related to risk management and information-sharing investments.

It is necessary to highlight that the Chamber supports CISA. Compared with S. 456, CISA offers a more dynamic approach to sharing cybersecurity threat data among multiple business and Government partners, coupled with stronger protections. CISA would go the furthest in helping businesses, including critical infrastructure, defend information systems against cyber attacks. Businesses would likely share and receive CTIs and countermeasures and monitor their networks on a broader scale and more confidently because CISA grants stronger liability protections and better policy tools.

Organizing roundtables with local chambers and growing market solutions. The Chamber is planning more cyber roundtables in 2015. Last year, the Chamber organized roundtable events with State and local chambers in Chicago, Illinois (May 22); Austin, Texas (July 10); Everett, Washington (September 23); and Phoenix, Arizona (October 8) prior to the Chamber's Third Annual Cybersecurity Summit on October 28.

Leading member sponsors of the campaign were American Express, Dell, and Splunk. Other sponsors were the American Gas Association, Boeing, the Edison Electric Institute, Exelon, HID Global, Microsoft, Oracle, and Pepco Holdings, Inc., and *The Wall Street Journal.*

Each roundtable featured cybersecurity principals from the White House, DHS, NIST, and local FBI and Secret Service officials. The Chamber and its partners urged businesses to adopt fundamental internet security practices to reduce network and system weaknesses and make the price of successful hacking increasingly steep. The Chamber also urged businesses to improve their cyber risk management processes.

All businesses should understand common on-line threats that can lead them to become victims of cyber crime. Using the framework and similar risk management tools, such as the Chamber's *Internet Security Essentials for Business 2.0* guide-

[11] *www.justice.gov/opa/pr/justice-department-federal-trade-commission-issue-antitrust-policy-statement-sharing.*
[12] CISA 2015 and S. 456 define cyber threat indicators (CTIs) in section 2 of their respective bills.

book,[13] is ultimately about making your business more secure and resilient. The Chamber encourages businesses to report cyber incidents. Perfect on-line security is unattainable, even for large businesses. Innovative solutions are regularly being brought to market because cyber threats are always changing. Businesses should report cyber incidents and on-line crime to their FBI or Secret Service field offices.

Increasing public awareness of the framework. The Chamber urges policymakers to commit greater resources over the next several years to growing awareness of the framework and risk-based solutions through a National education campaign. A broad-based campaign involving Federal, State, and local governments and multiple sectors of the U.S. economy would spur greater awareness of cyber threats and aggregate demand for market-driven cyber solutions.

The Chamber believes that Government—particularly independent agencies—should devote their limited time and resources to assisting resource-strapped enterprises, not trying to flex their existing regulatory authority. After all, while businesses are working to detect, prevent, and mitigate cyber attacks originating from sophisticated criminal syndicates or foreign powers, they should not have to worry about regulatory or legal sanctions.

Engaging law enforcement. The Chamber plans to continue its close contact with the FBI and the Secret Service to build trusted public-private relationships, which are essential to confirming a crime and beginning criminal investigations. The Chamber encourages businesses to partner with law enforcement before, during, and after a cyber incident. FBI and Secret Service officials have participated in each of the Chamber's roundtables.

Harmonizing cybersecurity regulations. Information-security requirements should not be cumulative. The Chamber believes it is valuable that agencies and departments are urged under the E.O. to report to the Office of Management and Budget any critical infrastructure subject to "ineffective, conflicting, or excessively burdensome cybersecurity requirements." The Chamber urges the administration and Congress to prioritize eliminating burdensome regulations on businesses. One solution could entail giving businesses credit for information security regimes that exist in their respective sectors.[14] It is positive that Michael Daniel, the administration's lead cyber official, has made harmonizing existing cyber regulations with the framework a priority.

Raising adversaries' costs through deterrence. The Chamber is reviewing actions that businesses and Government can take to deter nefarious actors that threaten to empty bank accounts, steal trade secrets, or damage vital infrastructures. While our organization has not formally endorsed the report, the U.S. Department of State's International Security Advisory Board (ISAB) issued in July draft recommendations regarding cooperation and deterrence in cyberspace.

The ISAB's recommendations—including cooperating on crime as a first step, exploring global consensus on the rules of the road, enhancing governments' situational awareness through information sharing, combating IP theft, expanding education and capacity building, promoting attribution and prosecution, and leading by example—are sensible and worthy of further review by cybersecurity stakeholders.[15]

The Chamber believes that the United States needs to coherently shift the costs associated with cyber attacks in ways that are legal, swift, and proportionate relative to the risks and threats. Policymakers need to help the law enforcement community, which is a key asset to the business community but numerically overmatched compared with illicit hackers.[16]

Making incentives work. In an April 2013 letter to NIST regarding businesses' use of the framework and the role of incentives, the Chamber provides its views on extending liability protections related to information-sharing legislation, a safe harbor related to using the framework, SAFETY Act applicability to the framework; elimi-

[13] The booklet is available free for downloading at *www.uschamber.com/issue-brief/internet-security-essentials-business-20.*

[14] The business community already complies with multiple information security rules. Among the regulatory requirements impacting businesses of all sizes are the Chemical Facilities Anti-Terrorism Standards (CFATS), the Federal Energy Regulatory Commission—North American Reliability Corporation Critical Information Protection (FERC–NERC CIP) standards, the Gramm-Leach-Bliley Act (GLBA), the Health Insurance Portability and Accountability Act (HIPAA), and the Sarbanes-Oxley (SOX) Act. The Securities and Exchange Commission (SEC) issued guidance in October 2011 outlining how and when companies should report hacking incidents and cybersecurity risks. Corporations also comply with many non-U.S. requirements, which add to the regulatory mix.

[15] The ISAB report is available at *www.state.gov/documents/organization/229235.pdf.*

[16] The Chamber argued for a clear cyber deterrence strategy in its December 2013 letter to NIST on the framework. See *http://csrc.nist.gov/cyberframework/framework_comments/20131213_ann_beauchesne_uschamber.pdf.*

nating cybersecurity regulations, leveraging Federal procurement, and making the research and development (R&D) tax credit permanent.[17]

The Chamber appreciates that the administration is assessing a mix of incentives that could induce businesses to use the framework.[18] However, in the Chamber's view, it is imperative that the administration, independent agencies, and lawmakers extend to companies the assurance that the cybersecurity framework and any actions taken in relation to it remain collaborative, flexible, and innovative over the long term. The Chamber believes that the presence of these qualities, or the lack thereof, would be a key determinant to use of the framework by U.S. critical infrastructure as well as businesses generally.

ROADMAP FOR THE FUTURE OF THE CYBERSECURITY FRAMEWORK

In February 2014, NIST released a *Roadmap* to accompany the framework. The *Roadmap* outlines further areas for possible "development, alignment, and collaboration."[19] The Chamber noted in an October 2014 letter to NIST some key areas that it sees as needing more attention. The Chamber would highlight for the committee the importance of aligning international cybersecurity regimes with the framework.

Many Chamber members operate globally and appreciate that NIST has been actively meeting with foreign governments urging them to embrace the framework. Like NIST, the Chamber believes that efforts to improve the cybersecurity of the public and private sectors should reflect the borderless and interconnected nature of our digital environment.

Standards, guidance, and best practices relevant to cybersecurity are typically industry-driven and adopted on a voluntary basis; they are most effective when developed and recognized globally. Such an approach would avoid burdening multinational enterprises with the requirements of multiple, and often conflicting, jurisdictions.[20] The administration should organize opportunities for stakeholders to participate in multinational discussions. The Chamber encourages the Federal Government to work with international partners and believes that these discussions should be stakeholder-driven and occur on a routine basis.

PASSING AN INDUSTRY-SUPPORTED INFORMATION-SHARING BILL IS THE CHAMBER'S TOP CYBER LEGISLATIVE GOAL IN 2015

Cyber attacks aimed at U.S. businesses and Government entities are being launched from various sources, including sophisticated hackers, organized crime, and state-sponsored groups. These attacks are advancing in scope and complexity. Most policymakers and practitioners appreciate that the intent of legislation is not to spur more information sharing for its own sake. Rather, the goal is to help companies achieve timely and actionable situational awareness to improve the business community's and the Nation's detection, mitigation, and response capabilities.

Additional positive side effects of enacting cyber information-sharing legislation include strengthening the security of personal information that is maintained on company networks and systems and increasing costs on nefarious actors. The bill would also complement the NIST framework, which many industry associations and companies are embracing and promoting with their business partners. Congressional action on cybersecurity information-sharing legislation cannot come quickly enough.

Mr. RATCLIFFE. Thank you, Mr. Eggers.

It is my understanding that votes have been called. We expect to return roughly 10 minutes after the last vote. So, without objection, the subcommittee is in recess subject to the call of the Chairman.

[Recess.]

---

[17] The letter is available at *www.ntia.doc.gov/files/ntia/29apr13_chamber_comments.pdf*.

[18] See *www.whitehouse.gov/blog/2013/08/06/incentives-support-adoption-cybersecurity-framework*.

[19] The Roadmap is available at *www.nist.gov/cyberframework/upload/roadmap-021214.pdf*.

[20] The Chamber sent a letter in September 2013 to Dr. Andreas Schwab, member of the European Parliament's Internal Market and Consumer Protection Committee, recommending amendments to the proposed European Union (E.U.) cybersecurity directive. The Chamber argues that cybersecurity and resilience are best achieved when organizations follow voluntary global standards and industry-driven practices.

Mr. RATCLIFFE. Appreciate everyone's patience. We're accommo-
dating with the weather, and I think we're going to have some
Members return. But I want to continue with everyone's testimony.

So I appreciate, Mr. Eggers, your testimony.

Next we would love to hear from Ms. Callahan.

TESTIMONY OF MARY ELLEN CALLAHAN, JENNER & BLOCK, FORMER CHIEF PRIVACY OFFICER, U.S. DEPARTMENT OF HOMELAND SECURITY

Ms. CALLAHAN. Thank you, sir.

Good afternoon, Chairman Ratcliffe. Thank you for the opportunity to appear before you today.

My name is Mary Ellen Callahan, and I'm a partner at the law
firm of Jenner & Block, where I chair the privacy and information
governance practice. From 2009 to 2012, I served as the Chief Privacy Officer of the U.S. Department of Homeland Security. I'm appearing before this committee in my personal capacity.

Cybersecurity information sharing is vital to protect private- and
public-sector assets. In order to prepare for disclosing cybersecurity
threat indicators, however, to the other entities in the cybersecurity ecosystem, the information sharing with the Government must
meet certain standards to address industry interests and needs.

There are six factors that are crucial for establishing robust effective private-sector information sharing with the Government:

First, the Government must establish and implement legitimate
privacy safeguards.

Second, clearly-established controls must be placed on what the
Government does with that shared information.

Third, the controls must include civilian interface with the private sector, not just as an intake center, but for all communications
and coordination related to cybersecurity information sharing.

Fourth, a value proposition for the information sharing must be
established.

Fifth, liability limitations must be provided both civilly and
criminally.

Finally, the Congress should expressly provide the Privacy and
Civil Liberties Oversight Board with oversight authority over cybersecurity, including information sharing.

It is unfortunate that the 2015 Executive Order did not elaborate
on the necessary privacy and civil liberties protections, particularly
with regard to private-sector information sharing.

Nonetheless, the DHS Privacy Officer and Office for Civil Rights
and Civil Liberties can address those private-sector concerns, including with the intersection of the Information Sharing and Analysis Organizations, or ISAOs.

DHS has been quite transparent about its cybersecurity capac-
ities and privacy protections starting from the time when Mr. Garcia was at Homeland Security. This work will assist DHS in establishing deeper relations with the new and existing ISAOs.

In addition, as this subcommittee knows, the DHS Chief Privacy
Officer has unique investigatory authorities. Therefore, in the
event that something went awry in the future, the Chief Privacy
Officer can investigate these activities. That authority may be of

interest to the private companies and ISAOs as more private information starts to flow into the Government.

There are three categories of information that companies may provide when sharing cybersecurity threat indicators: Information directly associated the cyber threat; information related to the cyber threat; and information incidentally retained when sharing the threat indicators themselves.

To limit the amount of incidentally retained and related information being shared, companies should implement strict data minimization standards. Frequently, however, it may not be evident upon initial sharing which information is directly associated with the threat and which information is either incidentally retained or only related to the cyber threat. Therefore, more information than necessary may be shared.

As a result, the Federal Government should implement a secondary data minimization review and limit any sharing of information only to the information directly associated with the threat.

In certain discussions, there have been recommendations to share all cybersecurity threat information, including the related and incidentally-retained information, as soon as possible with all Government entities. This is ill-advised.

If such sharing were to occur, each agency would need to re-analyze the information to determine what is relevant and what is not. If there is a requirement to immediately share, then more information than necessary will be shared throughout the Government.

Wide-spread sharing of related or incidentally-retained information will chill information sharing generally. Companies will not want their non-cyber-threat information shared widely, even if there are use limitations. To be clear, use limitations must be placed to provide guidance to the Government and necessary comfort to the sharing companies.

The use of private-sector shared information must be cabined to only include use for cybersecurity threat and response. Relatedly, the Federal Government, including intelligence agencies, should have limitations on what agencies can retain and for how long with regard to the shared information from companies.

Ensuring civilian control of the life cycle of cybersecurity information from the private sector is critical to comfort private companies before they share cybersecurity threat indicators in volume.

Critical infrastructure sectors in companies have had reservations about information being shared that may not only be used for informing other vulnerable entities, but also would have been used for investigations or National security without concomitant benefit.

The liability limitation is also important. Companies and ISAOs need to be comforted that the information they share will be appropriately protected.

Finally, the Privacy and Civil Liberties Oversight Board authority should be expanded to include oversight of cybersecurity activities, including information sharing with and from the private sector.

Thank you.

[The prepared statement of Ms. Callahan follows:]

PREPARED STATEMENT OF MARY ELLEN CALLAHAN

MARCH 4, 2015

Chairman Ratcliffe, Ranking Member Richmond, distinguished Members of the subcommittee, thank you for the opportunity to appear before you today. My name is Mary Ellen Callahan. I am a partner at the law firm of Jenner & Block, where I chair the Privacy and Information Governance Practice and counsel private-sector clients on integrating privacy and cybersecurity. From March 2009 to August 2012, I served as the chief privacy officer at the U.S. Department of Homeland Security (DHS or Department). I have worked as a privacy professional for 17 years and have National and international experience in integrating privacy into business and Government operations. I am appearing before this subcommittee in my personal capacity and not on behalf of any other entity.

Cybersecurity information sharing is vital to protect the private and public-sector assets. In order to prepare for disclosing cybersecurity threat indicators to other entities in the cybersecurity ecosystem, however, the information sharing with the Government must meet certain standards to address industry interests and needs.

In my testimony, I will address six factors that are crucial to establishing robust, effective private-sector information sharing with the Government. First and foremost, to encourage and facilitate private-sector information sharing, the Government must develop and implement legitimate privacy safeguards. Second, clearly-established controls must be placed on what the Government does with the shared information. Third, those controls must include identifying and empowering a civilian interface with the private sector on information sharing—not just as an intake center, but for all communications related to cybersecurity information sharing. The fourth necessary step is to establish the value proposition for information sharing; information sharing must be at an acceptable cost and provide minimal risk for the participants. Its companion point is to define clear and objective limitations on liability for companies that participate in information sharing—both civilly and criminally. And finally, Congress should expressly provide the Privacy and Civil Liberties Oversight Board with oversight authority over cybersecurity, including information sharing.

PRIVACY SAFEGUARDS ARE ESSENTIAL TO EFFECTIVE PRIVATE SECTOR INFORMATION SHARING

As Apple CEO Tim Cook noted at the Cybersecurity Summit last month, we have to protect our privacy rights or we will all face dire consequences. At the same Summit, President Obama concurred, saying, "When people go on-line, we shouldn't have to forfeit the basic privacy we're entitled to as Americans." However, the *Executive Order on Promoting Private Sector Cybersecurity Information Sharing* does not include a comprehensive privacy and civil liberties framework relating to private-sector sharing, instead focusing only on the intra-Government sharing, instructing agencies to work with their Senior Agency Officials for Privacy (SAOPs) to ensure that appropriate internal privacy protections are in place.

This decentralized and Government-only approach is flawed in two ways. Following the 2013 Executive Order on Improving Cybersecurity, each of the SAOPs for the major agencies prepared their assessments of how they were complying with privacy and civil liberties protections in department-to-department sharing. The detail and level of analysis by the SAOPs differed greatly. Having a decentralized assessment of privacy impacts, including how to intersect with the private sector, will delay the implementation of adequate privacy protections, and will not instill confidence from the private sector. Furthermore, this decentralized approach does not need to take place under the 2015 Executive Order—because DHS has already has an existing infrastructure in place, and it has been identified as the key department in this private-sector information-sharing exercise.

It is unfortunate that the 2015 Executive Order did not elaborate on the necessary privacy and civil liberties protections, particularly with regard to private-sector information sharing. Nonetheless, the DHS Privacy Office and Office for Civil Rights and Civil Liberties can lead these inter-agency efforts to address private-sector concerns, including with the intersection of Information Sharing and Analysis Organizations (ISAOs).

Without a White House-based privacy policy official, the DHS Chief Privacy Officer frequently serves as de facto privacy policy leadership between and among the departments and agencies. As I testified before this subcommittee in April 2013, DHS has taken multiple steps to integrate cybersecurity and privacy as part of the Department's cybersecurity mission. DHS has thoroughly integrated the Fair Information Practice Principles (FIPPs) into its cybersecurity programs. The FIPPS are the "widely accepted framework of defining principles to be used in the evaluation and consideration of systems, processes, or programs that affect individual privacy."[1]

DHS has been quite transparent about its cybersecurity capabilities. As discussed below, transparency is an important tenet under the FIPPs and an important cornerstone to encourage industry participation. DHS has published several Privacy Impact Assessments (PIAs) detailing pilot programs and information sharing among and between Government entities as well as with private companies that have signed Cooperative Research and Development Agreements (CRADAs). This work will assist DHS in establishing deeper relationships with new and existing ISAOs.

The Department already has skilled, dedicated privacy professionals who can help navigate the privacy protections needed for effective information sharing, with multiple cyber privacy professionals on staff. These individuals focus on integrating the FIPPs of purpose specification, data minimization, use limitation, data quality and integrity and security systematically into all DHS cybersecurity activities.

As part of its mission to implement the FIPPs and to integrate privacy protections into DHS cybersecurity activities, DHS privacy professionals review and provide comments and insight into cybersecurity Standard Operating Procedures (SOPs) (including protocols for human analysis and retention of cyber alerts, signatures, and indicators for minimization of information that could be personally identifiable information), statements of work, contracts, and international cyber information-sharing agreements. The DHS cyber privacy professionals review all of the CRADAs signed with private companies.

An important tenet of the FIPPs is the concept of accountability—periodically reviewing and confirming that the privacy protections initially embedded into any program remain relevant and that those protections are implemented.

While I was DHS Chief Privacy Officer, I instituted "Privacy Compliance Reviews" (PCRs) to confirm the accountability of several of DHS's programs.[2] We designed the PCR to improve a program's ability to comply with assurances made in PIAs, System of Records Notices, and formal information-sharing agreements. The Office conducts PCRs of on-going DHS programs with program staff to ascertain how required privacy protections are being implemented and to identify areas for improvement.

Given the importance of the DHS mission in cybersecurity, the DHS Privacy Office conducted a Privacy Compliance Review in late 2011, publishing it in early 2012.[3] The DHS Privacy Office found the DHS cybersecurity entities generally complied with the privacy requirements in the relevant Privacy Impact Assessments. Specifically, the DHS cybersecurity entities fully complied with collecting information, using information, internal and external sharing with Federal agencies and accountability requirements.

In addition, as this subcommittee knows, the DHS chief privacy officer has unique investigatory authorities. Therefore, in the unlikely event that something went awry in the future, the Chief Privacy Officer can investigate those activities.[4] This investigatory authority may be of interest to the private companies and ISAOs as more private information starts to flow into the Government.

The procedures, staffing, accountability and integration into the relationships with private-sector entities through CRADAs demonstrate the way in which privacy protections are integrated throughout the DHS cybersecurity program. A framework is in place to address privacy and civil liberties issues for private-sector information sharing, and DHS is well-positioned to extend those privacy protections to private-sector information sharing on a larger scale.

ESTABLISH APPROPRIATE LIMITATIONS ON INFORMATION SHARING

Consistent with the FIPPs and private-sector company expectations, there must be clearly-defined controls associated with the cybersecurity threat indicators and the related information.

As the DHS portion of the 2013 Executive Order report noted, there are at least three categories of information that companies may provide when sharing cybersecurity threat indicators—information directly associated with the cybersecurity

---

[1] The Fair Information Practice Principles as articulated in *National Strategy for Trusted Identities in Cyberspace*, April 2011, available at: *http://www.whitehouse.gov/sites/default/files/rss_viewer/NSTICstrategy_041511.pdf*

[2] See DHS *Privacy Office Annual Report*, July 2011–June 2012 at 39–40 for a detailed discussion of Privacy Compliance Reviews.

[3] Privacy Compliance Review of the EINSTEIN Program, January 3, 2012, available at: *http://www.dhs.gov/xlibrary/assets/privacy/privacy_privcomrev_nppd_ein.pdf*.

[4] 6 U.S.C. § 142(b). See DHS *Privacy Office Annual Report*, July 2011–June 2012 at 40 for a discussion of the DHS chief privacy officer investigatory authorities.

threat, information related to the cyber threat, and information incidentally retained when sharing the threat indicators themselves.[5]

To limit the amount of incidentally retained and related information being shared, companies should implement strict data minimization standards. Frequently, however, it may not be evident upon initial sharing—especially because time may be of the essence—which information is directly associated with the cybersecurity threat and which information is either incidentally retained or only related to the cyber threat. Therefore, more information than necessary may be shared. As a result, the Federal Government/DHS should implement a secondary data minimization review and limit any sharing of information only to the information directly associated with the cyber threat.

In certain discussions, there are recommendations to share all cybersecurity threat information—including the related and incidentally-retained information—as soon as possible with all Government entities. This is ill-advised, for a few reasons. First, this approach does not assist the other entities in identifying the relevant information and requires each agency to re-analyze the information to determine what is relevant and what is not. That is inefficient. Instead, sharing immediately shifts the burden of implementation and analysis to every entity and decentralizes the skill set. If there is a requirement to immediately share, then more information than necessary—and possibly inaccurate information—will be shared throughout the Government. For these two reasons, the experts at DHS should first parse the information and apply data minimization principles to allow other agencies to respond quickly to the threat itself, rather than weeding through potentially disparate layers of information. The same principle of double data minimization applies to information sharing between and among companies.

Wide-spread sharing of related or incidentally-retained information will chill information sharing generally. Companies will not want their non-cyber information shared widely, even if there are use limitations. Providing anonymity for producers (especially private companies)—allowing them an environment to share safely without fear of backlash regarding their vulnerabilities—is vital to encourage cooperation. Companies are legitimately concerned that their valuable trade secrets or business-sensitive information may be available to the Government and their competitors if the non-cyber threat indicators are not minimized.

Even if cyber threat indicators are judiciously shared, use limitations related to the shared information must be in place. In addition to the liability limitations discussed below, the use of private sector-shared information must be cabined to include only use for cybersecurity threat and response. Relatedly, the Federal Government (including intelligence agencies) should have limitations on what agencies can retain and for how long with regard to the unique information from companies, rather than the distilled threat indicators.

CIVILIAN CONTROL OF THE CYBERSECURITY INFORMATION SHARING IS CRUCIAL TO ENCOURAGE PRIVATE INFORMATION SHARING

Ensuring civilian control of the life cycle of cybersecurity information from the private sector is critical to comfort private companies before they share cyber threat indicators in volume. Critical infrastructure sectors and companies have reservations that information being shared may not only be used to inform other vulnerable entities, but also would be used for investigations or National security, without any other concomitant benefit. The Executive Order is silent on the issue of civilian control for the life cycle of the private-sector relationship, but that control is crucial to the development of repeatable, consistent information sharing.

Identifying DHS as the private-sector interface is vital to placate these concerns. This committee began this process with the legislative establishment of the National Cybersecurity and Communications Integration Center (NCCIC) in 2014 through the National Cybersecurity Protection Act. DHS must continue to be the primary interface with the private sector, and must not just be seen as a pass-through to the intelligence community.

As noted above, DHS has been transparent about its cybersecurity activities, which is imperative to develop credentials and credibility with the private sector. Now that NCCIC has been identified as the leading agency, any information sharing must go through it. As Assistant Secretary Andy Ozment reported to this committee in February, NCCIC received 97,000 incident reports, released 12,000 actionable cyber alerts or warnings and responded to 115 cyber incidents last year. These sta-

---

[5] *Executive Order 13636 Privacy and Civil Liberties Assessment Report 2014*, available at: *http://www.dhs.gov/sites/default/files/publications/2014-privacy-and-civil-liberties-assessment-report.pdf*

tistics demonstrate that DHS is maturing. As a civilian agency, it is well-positioned to liaise between private companies and the Government.

INFORMATION SHARING MUST NOT THREATEN COMPANIES

Information sharing must be at an acceptable cost and, therefore, provide minimal risk for the participants. If participants believe they will be targeted by attackers by sharing information, such as configurations, vulnerabilities, or even the fact that they have been targeted, they will not be willing to share information.

DHS has received thorough advice—including from private-sector representatives and advocates—as part of its Federal Advisory Committee Act privacy committee, the Data Privacy and Integrity Advisory Committee. The DPIAC issued a significant advisory paper for DHS to consider when implementing information-sharing pilots and programs with other entities, including the private sector.[6] The report addresses two important questions in privacy and cybersecurity: "What specific privacy protections should DHS consider when sharing information from a cybersecurity pilot project with other agencies?" and "What privacy considerations should DHS include in evaluating the effectiveness of cybersecurity pilots?" This type of advice helps DHS design systems to avoid antagonizing companies and ISAOs and comfort them they will not somehow be punished for participating.

LIMITATIONS ON LIABILITY MUST BE CLEARLY DEFINED

The issue of liability limitations has been discussed at length during the pendency of the cybersecurity legislation. It obviously is an important issue for companies, and it needs to be resolved appropriately in order to encourage information sharing. With that said, having clearly-defined limitations may help companies even more than having a "notwithstanding any other law" blanket exception.

The liability limitation must address at least two aspects directly. First, the shared information cannot be shared with other agencies and then used in a civil or criminal enforcement action against the sharing company. That is crucial. Furthermore, the shared information should not be used in civil or criminal enforcement actions against a third party who is not the cyber attacker—namely, if shared information contains damning information either about the sharing company or a third-party company, the Government's awareness of that information cannot lead to enforcement.

Furthermore, companies and ISAOs need to be comforted that the information they share will be appropriately protected. The DHS transparency on its systems will hopefully ameliorate that concern.

The anti-trust concerns raised in earlier Congresses have waned in light of the Joint Department of Justice/Federal Trade Commission Statement *Antitrust Policy Statement on Sharing of Cybersecurity Information.*[7] Nonetheless, more clarity, particularly vis-á-vis inter-company sharing, will induce more information sharing.

PRIVACY AND CIVIL LIBERTIES OVERSIGHT BOARD SHOULD BE GRANTED OVERSIGHT AUTHORITY OVER CYBERSECURITY INFORMATION SHARING

The Privacy and Civil Liberties Oversight Board (PCLOB) serves an important oversight function on intelligence and National security activities related to terrorism. The PCLOB's authority should be expanded to include oversight on cybersecurity activities, including information sharing with and from the private sector. This addition will further bolster the FIPPs throughout the cyber information-sharing life cycle, and will provide additional oversight capacity over the collection, use, sharing, and retention of private-sector information.

Thank you for the opportunity to appear before this subcommittee this afternoon. I would be happy to take any questions you may have.

Mr. RATCLIFFE. Thank you, Ms. Callahan.

The Chairman now recognizes Mr. Garcia to testify.

---

[6] *Report from the Cyber Subcommittee to the Data Privacy and Integrity Advisory Committee (DPIAC) on Privacy and Cybersecurity Pilots,* Submitted by the DPIAC Cybersecurity Subcommittee, November 2012, available at: *http://www.dhs.gov/sites/default/files/publications/privacy/DPIAC/dpiac_cyberpilots_10_29_2012.pdf.*

[7] *http://www.justice.gov/atr/public/guidelines/305027.pdf.*

TESTIMONY OF GREGORY T. GARCIA, EXECUTIVE DIRECTOR, FINANCIAL SERVICES SECTOR COORDINATING COUNCIL

Mr. GARCIA. Thank you, Mr. Chairman. Thanks for the opportunity to address the subcommittee about the President's information-sharing Executive Order.

The Financial Services Sector Coordinating Council, or FSSCC, was establishes in 2002. It involves 65 of the largest financial services providers and their industry associations. Its mission is to coordinate sector-wide efforts to strengthen the resiliency of the financial services sector against threats to the Nation's critical infrastructure. So we're focused on the critical infrastructure sector.

In practice, this means that we work with Government and other partners to address information-sharing content and procedures, incident response, cyber and operational risk management best practices, and appropriate policy enhancements to support the above objectives.

We've learned over the years that strong risk management requires participating in communities of trust that share information on cyber and physical threats, vulnerabilities, and incidents. This is based on the simple concept of strength in numbers, the neighborhood watch, shared situational awareness.

While the FSSCC focuses on longer-term trends and strategy, our sector's operational arm is the Financial Services Information Sharing and Analysis Center, or FS–ISAC. The FS–ISAC participates in many information-sharing programs. One key partner that you mentioned in your opening statement is the National Cybersecurity and Communications Integration Center, or NCCIC.

The NCCIC is a hub for sharing information about cyber and communications incidents across sectors, and the financial sector has a seat on the NCCIC watch floor. The industry-sector officials that serve on the NCCIC are cleared at the Top Secret level. So they attend daily briefs and other NCCIC meetings about threats, vulnerabilities, and incidents affecting the financial sector.

Within the sector, FS–ISAC manages a formal structure for collecting, analyzing, and sharing actionable intelligence and best practices among members and the sector, as well as with our industry, Government, and law enforcement partners. I'll be happy to talk about all of that in detail during Q and A about how we do that.

The sector continues to make progress on the speed and reliability of its information-sharing efforts. Late last year, for example, the financial sector announced a new automated threat-sharing capability called Soltra Edge. This uses open standards funded by DHS that facilitate automated machine-to-machine information sharing.

It helps our industry increase the speed, scale, and accuracy of information sharing, and it accelerates the time to resolution. It can be used by any sectors and with any sectors or information-sharing groups. So this is a way of complimenting human-to-human sharing by using machine-to-machine whenever possible.

So the point is the financial sector has a very robust information-sharing environment among ourselves and with the Government and we're always working to improve it.

So let me just spend the final moments of my statement discussing the President's Executive Order on private-sector information sharing.

In our view, the administration's Executive Action is a positive step. We expect it has the potential to increase the volume and quality of actionable and timely cybersecurity information. We offer a few observations that can inform implementation of the order.

First, as the sharing and use of Classified information can improve our response capability, it's important that the clearance process for critical sectors like ours is fast and efficient. The Executive Order supports this goal by enhancing DHS's involvement in the clearance process. This can help accelerate the security clearance process for critical sector owners and operators.

Also, in general, we support the creation of the ISAOs, Information Sharing Analysis Organizations. This can be a way for non-critical sector groups to share cybersecurity information and coordinate analysis and response.

We understand that the impetus for the ISAO proposal was to raise awareness for stakeholder groups looking to coalesce around joint information-sharing objectives, and we believe that the ISAO standards development process should build on the strong foundation laid by the ISACs.

We caveat, however, that ISACs, as distinct from ISAOs, must retain their special partnership status with the Government, given their broad sector representation and a strong cadre of operational support with security clearances.

Certain important principles need to be kept in mind for the standards development process. Sharing is successful within communities of trust when there are clear and enforced information-handling rules.

Information sharing is not a competitive sport. Operational standards should incentivize federated information-sharing. Intelligence needs to be fused across trust communities, not diffused or siloed.

Government processes for collecting, analyzing, and packaging intelligence for private-sector consumption must be streamlined and transparent. Indeed, the 2013 Executive Order directs the Government to do just that.

In anticipating the potential for heavy demands from a proliferation of ISAOs, the NCCIC should prioritize its resources and engagements according to established criteria. They'll need to consider Government capacity to effectively serve critical sector constituents in steady-state and surge mode. They need to consider the reach those stakeholders have into their sectors and the effectiveness of their capabilities.

It's also important that the ISAO standards development process be collaborative, open, and transparent. The process managed during the development of the NIST cybersecurity framework, for example, is an excellent example of this principle.

Okay. Mr. Chairman, that concludes my oral remarks. I'll be happy to answer questions.

[The prepared statement of Mr. Garcia follows:]

PREPARED STATEMENT OF GREGORY T. GARCIA

MARCH 4, 2015

Chairman Ratcliffe, Ranking Member Richmond, and Members of the sub-committee, thank you for this opportunity to address the subcommittee about the President's information sharing Executive Order.

My name is Gregory T. Garcia. I am executive director of the Financial Services Sector Coordinating Council (FSSCC), which was established in 2002 and involves 65 of the largest financial services providers and industry associations representing clearinghouses, commercial banks, credit card networks and credit rating agencies, exchanges/electronic communication networks, financial advisory services, insurance companies, financial utilities, Government-sponsored enterprises, investment banks, merchants, retail banks, and electronic payment firms.

FSSCC MISSION

The mission of the FSSCC is to strengthen the resiliency of the financial services sector against attacks and other threats to the Nation's critical infrastructure by proactively identifying threats and promoting protection, driving preparedness, collaborating with the Federal Government, and coordinating crisis response for the benefit of the financial services sector, consumers and the Nation's economic security. During the past decade, this strategic partnership has continued to grow, in terms of both the size and commitment of its membership and the breadth of issues it addresses. Members volunteer their time and resources to FSSCC with a sense of responsibility to the broader sector, financial consumers and the Nation.

In simplest terms, members of the FSSCC assess security and resiliency trends and policy developments affecting our critical financial infrastructure, and coordinate among ourselves and with our partners to develop a consolidated point of view and coherent strategy for dealing with those issues.

Accordingly, our sector's primary objectives are to:

1. Implement and maintain structured routines for sharing timely and actionable information related to cyber and physical threats and vulnerabilities among firms, across sectors of industry, and between the private sector and Government.

2. Improve risk management capabilities and the security posture of firms across the financial sector and the service providers they rely on by encouraging the development and use of common approaches and best practices.

3. Collaborate with homeland security, law enforcement and intelligence communities, financial regulatory authorities, other sectors of industry, and international partners to respond to and recover from significant incidents.

4. Discuss policy and regulatory initiatives that advance infrastructure resiliency and security priorities through robust coordination between Government and industry.

To achieve these objectives we partner with the Department of Treasury, DHS, law enforcement, and financial regulatory agencies forming our Government Coordinating Council counterpart—called the Financial and Banking Information Infrastructure Committee (FBIIC).

Rolling up into those broad objectives are numerous initiatives undertaken collaboratively within this public-private partnership, including committee-organized workstreams to, for example:

- improve information-sharing content and procedures between Government and the sector;
- conduct joint exercises to test our resiliency and information-sharing procedures under differing scenarios;
- prioritize critical infrastructure protection research and development funding needs;
- engage with other critical sectors and international partners to better understand and leverage our interdependencies;
- advocate broad adoption of the NIST Cybersecurity Framework, including among small and mid-sized financial institutions across the country;
- develop best practices guidance for operational risk issues involving third-party risk, supply chain, and cyber insurance strategies.

We have learned over the years that a foundational element of any strong risk management strategy for cyber and physical protection involves participation in communities of trust that share information related to threats, vulnerabilities, and incidents affecting those communities. That foundation is based on the simple concepts of strength in numbers, the neighborhood watch, and shared situational awareness.

To achieve this goal, public and private-sector partners exchange data and contextual information about specific incidents and longer-term trends and developments. Sharing this information helps to prevent incidents from occurring and to reduce the risk of a successful incident at one firm later impacting another. These efforts increasingly focus on including smaller firms and include international partners.

Financial-sector stakeholders participate in information-sharing programs operated by the Department of Homeland Security. For example, the financial sector and Treasury Department maintain a presence within the National Cybersecurity and Communications Integration Center (NCCIC), which serves as a hub for sharing information related to cybersecurity and communications incidents across sectors, among other roles and responsibilities. The sector also works closely with the National Infrastructure Coordinating Center (NICC), which is the dedicated 24/7 coordination and information-sharing operations center that maintains situational awareness of the Nation's critical infrastructure for the Federal Government.

The financial sector benefits greatly from its close information-sharing relationship with law enforcement partners, including the Federal Bureau of Investigations and the United States Secret Service.

FS–ISAC INFORMATION-SHARING PROGRAMS AND OPERATIONS

For the financial sector, the primary community of trust for critical financial infrastructure protection is the Financial Services Information Sharing and Analysis Center, or FS–ISAC, which is the operational heartbeat of the FSSCC strategic body.

The FS–ISAC was formed in 1999 in response to the 1998 Presidential Decision Directive 63 (PDD 63), which called for the public and private sectors to work together to address cyber threats to the Nation's critical infrastructures. After 9/11, and in response to Homeland Security Presidential Directive 7 (and its 2013 successor, Presidential Policy Directive 21) and the Homeland Security Act, the FS–ISAC expanded its role to encompass physical threats to our sector.

The FS–ISAC is a 501(c)6 nonprofit organization and is funded entirely by its member firms and sponsors. In 2004, there were only 68 members of the FS–ISAC, mostly larger financial services firms. Since that time the membership has expanded to more than 5,000 organizations including commercial banks and credit unions of all sizes, brokerage firms, insurance companies, data security payments processors, and 24 trade associations representing virtually all of the U.S. financial services sector.

Since its founding, the FS–ISAC's operations and culture of trusted collaboration have evolved into what we believe is a successful model for how other industry sectors can organize themselves around this security imperative. The overall objective of the FS–ISAC is to protect the financial services sector against cyber and physical threats and risk. It acts as a trusted third party that provides anonymity to allow members to share threat, vulnerability, and incident information in a non-attributable and trusted manner. The FS–ISAC provides a formal structure for valuable and actionable information to be shared amongst members, the sector, and its industry and Government partners, which ultimately benefits the Nation. FS–ISAC information-sharing activities include:

- delivery of timely, relevant, and actionable cyber and physical email alerts from various sources distributed through the FS–ISAC Security Operations Center (SOC);
- an anonymous on-line submission capability to facilitate member sharing of threat, vulnerability, and incident information in a non-attributable and trusted manner;
- operation of email listservs supporting attributable information exchange by various special interest groups including the Financial Services Sector Coordinating Council (FSSCC), the FS–ISAC Threat Intelligence Committee, threat intelligence sharing open to the membership, the Payment Processors Information Sharing Council (PPISC), the Clearing House and Exchange Forum (CHEF), the Business Resilience Committee, and the Payments Risk Council;
- anonymous surveys that allow members to request information regarding security best practices at other organizations;
- bi-weekly threat information sharing calls for members and invited security/risk experts to discuss the latest threats, vulnerabilities, and incidents affecting the sector;
- emergency threat or incident notifications to all members using the Critical Infrastructure Notification System (CINS);
- emergency conference calls to share information with the membership and solicit input and collaboration;

- engagement with private security companies to identify threat information of relevance to the membership and the sector;
- participation in various cyber exercises such as those conducted by DHS (Cyber Storm I, II, and III) and support for FSSCC exercises such as CyberFIRE and Quantum Dawn;
- development of risk mitigation best practices, threat viewpoints and toolkits, and preparation of cybersecurity briefings and white papers;
- administration of Subject Matter Expert (SME) committees including the Threat Intelligence Committee and Business Resilience Committee, which: Provide in-depth analyses of risks to the sector, conduct technical, business, and operational impact assessments; determine the sector's cyber and physical threat level; and, recommend mitigation and remediation strategies and tactics;
- special projects to address specific risk issues such as the Account Takeover Task Force;
- document repositories for members to share information and documentation with other members;
- development and testing of crisis management procedures for the sector in collaboration with the FSSCC and other industry bodies;
- semi-annual member meetings and conferences; and
- on-line webinar presentations and regional outreach programs to educate organizations, including small- to medium-sized regional financial services firms, on threats, risks, and best practices.

FS–ISAC PARTNERSHIPS

The FS–ISAC works closely with various Government agencies including the U.S. Department of Treasury, Department of Homeland Security (DHS), Federal Reserve, Federal Financial Institutions Examination Council (FFIEC) regulatory agencies, United States Secret Service, Federal Bureau of Investigation (FBI), the intelligence community, and State and local governments.

In partnership with DHS, FS–ISAC 2 years ago became the third ISAC to participate in the National Cybersecurity and Communications Integration Center (NCCIC) watch floor. FS–ISAC representatives, cleared at the Top Secret/Sensitive Compartmented Information (TS/SCI) level, attend the daily briefs and other NCCIC meetings to share data information on threats, vulnerabilities, incidents, and potential or known impacts to the financial services sector. Our presence on the NCCIC floor has enhanced situational awareness and information sharing between the financial services sector and the Government, and there are numerous examples of success to illustrate this.

As part of this partnership, the FS–ISAC set up an email listserv with U.S. CERT where actionable incident, threat, and vulnerability information is shared in near-real time. This listserv allows FS–ISAC members to share directly with U.S. CERT and further facilitates the information sharing that is already occurring between FS–ISAC members and with the NCCIC watch floor or with other Government organizations.

In addition, FS–ISAC representatives sit on the Cyber Unified Coordination Group (Cyber UCG). This group was set up under authority of the National Cyber Incident Response Plan (NCIRP) and has been actively engaged in incident response. Cyber UCG's handling and communications with various sectors following the distributed denial of service (DDOS) attacks on the financial sector in late 2012 and early 2013 is one example of how this group is effective in facilitating relevant and actionable information sharing.

Consistent with the directives of Presidential Policy Directive 21 and Executive Order 13636 of 2014, the Treasury established the Cyber Intelligence Group (CIG) as part of the Office of Critical Infrastructure Protection and Compliance Policy. The CIG was established in response to a need identified by the financial sector for the Government to have a focal point for sharing cyber threat-related information with the sector. The CIG identifies and analyzes all-source intelligence on cyber threats to the financial sector; shares timely, actionable information that alerts the sector to threats and enables firms' prevention and mitigation efforts; and solicits feedback and information requirements from the sector.

Finally, it should be noted that the FS–ISAC and FSSCC have worked closely with its Government partners to obtain security clearances for key financial services sector personnel. These clearances have been used to brief the sector on new information security threats and have provided useful information for the sector to implement effective risk controls to combat these threats.

In addition, several membership subgroups meet regularly with their own circles of trust to share information, including: The Insurance Risk Council (IRC); the Community Institution Council (CIC) with hundreds of members from community banks and credit unions; and the Community Institution Toolkit Working Group with a mission to develop a framework and series of best practices to protect community institutions. This includes a mentoring program to assist community institutions just getting started with an IT security staff.

The FS–ISAC also works very closely with the other critical infrastructure sectors on an ISAC-to-ISAC basis as well as through the National Council of ISACs. Information about threats, incidents, and best practices is shared daily among the ISACs via ISAC analyst calls, and a cross-sector information-sharing platform. The ISACs also come together during a crisis to coordinate information and mitigations as applicable.

AUTOMATED THREAT INFORMATION SHARING

The sector continues to make significant progress toward increasing the speed and reliability of its information-sharing efforts through expanded use of DHS-funded open specifications, including Structured Threat Information eXchange (STIX™) and Trusted Automated eXchange of Indicator Information (TAXII™).

Late last year, the financial sector announced a new automated threat capability it created called "Soltra Edge", which is the result of a joint venture of the FS–ISAC and the Depository Trust and Clearing Corporation. This capability addresses a fundamental challenge in our information-sharing environment: Typically the time associated with chasing down any specific threat indicator is substantial. The challenge has been to help our industry increase the speed, scale, and accuracy of information sharing and accelerate time to resolution.

The Soltra Edge capability developed by the sector removes a huge burden of work for both large and small financial organizations, including those that rely on third parties for monitoring and incident response. It is designed for use by many parts of the critical infrastructure ecosystem, including the financial services sector, the health care sector, the energy sectors, transportation sectors, other ISACs, National and regional CERTs (Computer Emergency Response Teams) and vendors and services providers that serve these sectors.

Key goals of Soltra-Edge are to:
- Deliver an industry-created utility to automate threat intelligence sharing;
- Reduce response time from days/weeks/months to seconds/minutes;
- Deliver 10 times reduction in effort and cost to respond;
- Operate on the tenets of at-cost model and open standards (STIX, TAXII);
- Leverage DTCC scalability; FS–ISAC community & best practices;
- Provide a platform that can be extended to all sizes of financial services firms, other ISACs and industries;
- Enable integration with vendor solutions (firewalls, intrusion detection, antivirus, threat intelligence, etc.).

With these advancements, one organization's incident becomes everyone's defense at machine speed. We expect this automated solution to be a "go-to" resource to speed incident response across thousands of organizations in many countries within the next few years.

EXERCISES

The sector regularly tests its resilience through exercises to identify gaps and exercise processes related to information sharing. Efforts such as the annual "Cyber Attack against Payment Processes (CAPP)", "Quantum Dawn" and public/private exercises provide essential insight into our ability individually and collaboratively to respond to various attack scenarios.

In carrying out this information-sharing partnership, the financial sector and Government partners are committed to ensuring that individual privacy and civil liberties protections are incorporated into all activities, to include technical analysis, information sharing on threats, and incident response efforts.

THE PRESIDENT'S EXECUTIVE ORDER ON PROMOTING PRIVATE-SECTOR CYBERSECURITY INFORMATION SHARING

As discussed above, the Financial Services Sector Coordinating Council (FSSCC) considers strong collaboration and information sharing within the sector and with Government to be a critical element of cybersecurity risk management.

Thus, in alignment with the FS–ISAC's statement for the record by Denise Anderson, vice president of the FS–ISAC and chair of the National Council of ISACs, we applaud this administration's efforts to improve our cybersecurity information-sharing environment so that we can better anticipate, protect against, and respond to cyber threats. The administration's Executive Action is a positive step toward increasing the volume and quality of actionable and timely cybersecurity information.

With key Federal support from the Treasury Department as our Sector-Specific Agency, law enforcement and the Department of Homeland Security (DHS), our network defenders are better able to prepare for cyber threats when there is a consistent, reliable, and sustainable flow of actionable cybersecurity information and analysis, at both a Classified and Unclassified level.

We are making some progress toward this goal, but it has become increasingly necessary for appropriately-cleared representatives of critical sectors such as financial services to have access, and provide contributions, to Classified information that enables analysts and operators to take timely action to defend essential systems. Accordingly, the Executive Order's enhancement of DHS's role in accelerating the security clearance process for critical sector owners and operators is a clear indication of the administration's support for this public-private partnership.

In considering enhancements to this model, agility and innovation are essential for the operational resilience of critical sector functions. In this spirit, we support the creation of Information Sharing and Analysis Organizations (ISAOs) as a mechanism for all sectors, regions, and other stakeholder groups to share cybersecurity information and coordinate analysis and response.

While ISACs must retain their status as the Government's primary critical infrastructure partners given their mandate for broad sectoral representation, the development of ISAOs should be facilitated for stakeholder groups that require a collaborative cyber and physical threat information-sharing capability that builds on the strong foundation laid by the ISACs.

As the ISAO standards development process unfolds, the FSSCC believes certain principles must be upheld for structuring both the ISAOs themselves and the Government's interaction with them:

- Sharing of sensitive security information within and among communities of trust is successful when operational standards of practice establish clear and enforced information handling rules.
- Information sharing is not a competitive sport: While competition in innovation can improve technical capabilities, operational standards should incentivize federated information sharing. Threat and vulnerability intelligence needs to be fused across trust communities, not diffused or siloed.
- Government internal processes for collecting, analyzing, and packaging CIP intelligence for ISAC/ISAO consumption must be streamlined and transparent to maximize timeliness, accuracy, and relevance of actionable shared information. Indeed, Section 4 of EO 13636 directs the Government to improve its dissemination of cyber threat intelligence to the private sector, enabling entities to protect their networks. Full implementation of this directive is necessary to achieve the objectives of the President's information sharing Executive Order.
- To manage scarce resources, Government information-sharing mechanisms such as the National Cyber and Communications Integration Center (NCCIC) and the Treasury Department's Cyber Intelligence Group (CIG) should prioritize engagements with ISACs and ISAOs according to transparently-established impact criteria, such as Government capacity to effectively serve CIP constituents in steady-state and surge mode, the reach those CIP stakeholders have into their sectors, and the effectiveness of their capabilities.

It is also important that the process to develop the ISAO standards is collaborative, open, and transparent. The process managed by the National Institute of Standards and Technology (NIST) during the development of the NIST Cybersecurity Framework is an excellent example of the appropriate leveraging of private-sector input, knowledge, and experience to develop guidance that will primarily impact non-Governmental entities. We encourage DHS, as the implementing authority of the President's EO, to emulate the engagement model that NIST used to create and adopt their Cybersecurity Framework. The process worked.

Finally, for DHS to be successful implementing this EO and its many cybersecurity risk management and partnership authorities, it must be sufficiently resourced with the best analytical and technical capabilities, with a cadre of highly-qualified cybersecurity leaders and analytical teams to conduct its mission. There must be a concerted effort to recruit, retain, and maintain a world-class workforce that is able to assess cyber threats globally and help the private sector reduce risk to this Nation.

The FSSCC believes that, with the application of the principles discussed in this statement, the creation of ISAOs and their partnership agreements with DHS have the potential to complement the ISAC foundation and measurably improve cyber risk reduction for critical infrastructure and the National economy.

On the subject of legislation, Mr. Chairman, passing cyber threat information-sharing legislation that encourages more information sharing between the private sector and Government and within the private sector, with fewer concerns about liability, will have a positive operational impact on the security of the Nation's networks. This sector-wide position is articulated in detail in recent letters from leading financial services trade associations.

Mr. Chairman and Members of the committee, this concludes my testimony.

Mr. RATCLIFFE. Thank you, Mr. Garcia.

Mr. RATCLIFFE. The Chairman now recognizes Dr. Libicki.

STATEMENT OF MARTIN C. LIBICKI, THE RAND CORPORATION

Mr. LIBICKI. Good afternoon, Chairman Ratcliffe, Ranking Member Richmond, and distinguished Members of the subcommittee. My name is Martin Libicki from The RAND Corporation.

Thank you for the opportunity to testify today about the President's cybersecurity information-sharing proposal. As a general proposition, information sharing among defenders makes for a better defense.

Nevertheless, two concerns merit note. First, the current proposals do not address and may even exacerbate a cybersecurity divide. Second, an enormous amount of political energy is being dedicated to a point solution to a broad problem.

A cybersecurity divide exists between organizations, roughly speaking, large enough to afford their own chief information security officer and those that cannot.

ISAOs, for their part, are oriented towards organizations that can afford the membership fees. Unless other mechanisms to share information with the smaller organizations are bolstered, the latter are going to be left out of whatever information-sharing exists.

As for the narrower focus, several weeks ago President Obama said, "There's only one way to defend America from cyber threats, and that's Government and industry working together, sharing appropriate information." An associated Executive Order calls for "fostering the development and adoption of automated mechanisms for the sharing of information."

However, cybersecurity is so complex a challenge that not only is information sharing not the "only one way," but the model proposed for information sharing is not even the only one way to share information.

To explain why, let's note three models of information sharing.

In the first model, vulnerabilities in software are found by white hat hackers and the forensic specialists brought into the attention of the vendors. The vendors, when they receive this information, attack the vulnerabilities and generally fix them. This is a model that would lead to better software and can be encouraged by the Federal Government with a modest addition of funding and without having to pass any new laws.

In a second model, the collection and analysis of cyber attacks can shed light on what organizations could have done differently to have prevented or at least mitigated the effects of such attacks. Such sharing permits evidence-based assessments of alternative cybersecurity tools, techniques, and practices. This model can be encouraged by empowering organizations, such as NIST, and funding various R&D entities, such as the ARPAs and NSF, to build and disseminate a systematic body of knowledge on cybersecurity.

The first model results in better software. The second model results in better cybersecurity management. Organizations of all size can benefit from each.

The third model of information sharing, organizations are asked to report details of the attacks they have suffered, such as malware samples, attacker modus operandi, IP addresses, attack vectors, induced anomalies, social engineering methods and so on. These are used to profile specific threat actors so that the signatures of their activity can be fed to intrusion detection and prevention systems of organizations that happen to have them.

The usefulness of this third model, however, requires that four assumptions be true.

The first assumption is that most serious attacks come from specific black hat hacker groups who repeat their attacks often enough so that evidence from early attacks can be used to detect later ones.

The second assumption is that such groups maintain a consistent modus operandi that is constantly reused.

The third assumption is that such signatures can be shared in a timely manner, something that is complicated by the length of time—several months to a year—between when a typical advanced attack starts and when it is discovered.

The fourth assumption is that such signatures will not evolve over time, even if information sharing were to become so widespread that the failure to evolve on the part of hackers would doom their ability to compromise networks.

An analogy may be made to the anti-virus industry. The majors run very large information-gathering networks fed by inputs from sensors placed throughout the internet, but the anti-virus model has lost viability in the face of ever-shifting signatures and the tendency of attackers to test their malware against anti-virus suites before releasing them.

Granted, the threat-based information-sharing model, if substantiated, would not be totally useless. Not every black hat hacker group will be conscientiously altering its modus operandi, and forcing such groups to cluster their attacks or shift their attack vectors does mean more work for them.

Nevertheless, threat-based information sharing is no panacea, and, yet, efforts to achieve it have absorbed a disproportional share of the legislative and media bandwidth on the topic of cybersecurity policy, crowding out the consideration of alternative approaches. Hence, the basis for our concern.

I appreciate the opportunity to discuss this important topic, and I look forward to your questions.

[The prepared statement of Mr. Libicki follows:]

PREPARED STATEMENT OF MARTIN C. LIBICKI [1][2]

MARCH 4, 2015

Good morning, Chairman Ratcliffe, Ranking Member Richmond, and distinguished Members of the subcommittee. I thank you for the opportunity to testify today about the President's cybersecurity information-sharing proposal.

The President's initiatives to improve cybersecurity through information sharing are laudable. Information sharing can and should be an important element in efforts to ensure that defenders learn from each other faster than attackers learn from each other. The fact that attackers do learn from each other is something that we know from research that RAND conducted for a report released last year on cyber crime markets (Markets for Cybercrime Tools and Stolen Data: Hackers' Bazaar).

People have been calling for greater information sharing for almost 20 years, dating back to the formation of Information Sharing and Analysis Centers (ISACs) in the late 1990s and continuing through the recent reformulation of ISACs into Information Sharing and Analysis Organizations (ISAOs). Although more information is being shared, the President's initiatives are prompted by the perception that information sharing is not advancing fast enough. Those asked to share gain little directly from sharing and believe they face financial, reputational, and legal risks in doing so. As a result, legislation has been repeatedly introduced to facilitate the increased exchange of information—notably, I would argue, threat information. Without going into a detailed assessment of the privacy implications of such legislation, apart from noting that concerns have been raised, its purposes are nevertheless sound and its passage can help improve cybersecurity.

Two concerns, however, merit note. One is that the current proposals do not address, and may even exacerbate, the differences between the cybersecurity enjoyed by small- and medium-sized enterprises on the one hand and that enjoyed by large enterprises on the other: A cybersecurity divide. The second concern is that the current legislative proposals represent an enormous amount of political energy dedicated to what is actually a narrowly-focused point solution to the problem of cybersecurity when a much broader approach is required. Consider each concern in turn.

The cybersecurity divide exists roughly at the boundary between those organizations that are large enough to afford their own chief information security officer (CISO) and those that cannot. As a very rough estimate, though this varies by sector, organizations with more than 1,000 employees can afford to hire a CISO, and those that are smaller cannot. Organizations that cannot afford to employ a CISO can usually offer only generalized cybersecurity training for their employees (if they do so at all); must rely on commodity hardware and software, often deployed with default settings; make do with commercial network offerings such as routers; and use off-the-shelf firewall tools. Organizations that can afford to employ a CISO can offer and customize specialized training, can afford to optimize their hardware and software for cybersecurity, can purchase sophisticated cybersecurity tools, can hire information security analysts, and contract with third parties for additional cybersecurity services. Fortunately, cloud offerings can be and are tailored for organizations of all sizes, but this only represents a partial approach to cybersecurity and may introduce a few additional security problems of their own.

ISAOs, laudable as they may be, are oriented toward organizations that can afford their membership fees; at $10,000 a year, most small- and medium-sized organizations are priced out of that market. Consider the likelihood that these ISAO's become the primary—or worse, exclusive—conduit for information sharing between the Government and private organizations. If so—and in the absence of other mechanisms to share information with the broader public—the smaller organizations are going to be left out. Whatever advantage they reap from information-sharing rests on the hope that the existence of ISAOs as conduits for shared information does not detract from paths more suited to smaller enterprises.

The risks of exacerbating the cybersecurity divide are related to the problem of an overly narrow focus for information sharing associated with pending legislation.

---

[1] The opinions and conclusions expressed in this testimony are the author's alone and should not be interpreted as representing those of RAND or any of the sponsors of its research. This product is part of the RAND Corporation testimony series. RAND testimonies record testimony presented by RAND associates to Federal, State, or local legislative committees; Government-appointed commissions and panels; and private review and oversight bodies. The RAND Corporation is a nonprofit research organization providing objective analysis and effective solutions that address the challenges facing the public and private sectors around the world. RAND's publications do not necessarily reflect the opinions of its research clients and sponsors.

[2] TThis testimony is available for free download at http://www.rand.org/pubs/testimonies/CT425.html.

Several weeks ago, during the Cybersecurity Summit, President Obama said, "There's only one way to defend America from cyber threats, and that's Government and industry working together [and] sharing appropriate information." However, cybersecurity is not that elementary; there is no one unique way. Furthermore, the associated Executive Order calls for "fostering the development and adoption of automated mechanisms for the sharing of information." That being so, not only is information sharing not the "only one way" to improve cybersecurity, but the model proposed for information sharing is also not the "only one way" to share information.

To explain why requires stepping back to take a broader look at information sharing. Among the many types of information sharing, three merit note.

First is the process by which software vulnerabilities are brought to the attention of those who make and maintain software. A large percentage of all networks—particularly the more diligently-defended ones—are penetrated because their software contains vulnerabilities that have not been fixed, notably because the vendors have not discovered them. These are "zero-day vulnerabilities"; they permit "zero-day exploits." Software vulnerabilities in Java, Acrobat, Flash, and Microsoft Office products are commonly exploited to allow attackers to enter computer networks and systems (which is why users are warned not to click on suspect websites or open suspicious attachments). A large and growing community of researchers and white hat hackers are busy finding these vulnerabilities and reporting them to vendors. A related community examines actual cyber attacks to determine which vulnerabilities were exploited in order to serve the same end of fixing them. A world with fewer software vulnerabilities would be a safer world (although patches do no good until installed). Occasionally, software vendors confronted with a number of similar vulnerability reports about their products may find correlated architectural weaknesses in their offerings and make more fundamental changes. The Federal Government can do more to encourage and accelerate the process of finding software vulnerabilities with modest amounts of funding and without passing new legislation.

Second is the use of information sharing to improve cybersecurity practice. The collection and analysis of cyber attacks, both those that succeed and those that may be termed near-misses, can shed light on what organizations could have done differently to have prevented or at least mitigated the effects of such attacks. Such analysis can provide evidence-based assessments of the cost-effectiveness of alternative cybersecurity tools and techniques. Such an activity is already informally carried out to some extent at the worker level, especially among the information security community and disseminated through professional interaction. This should continue to be encouraged, and should trickle up to the C–Suite and managers. Such activity can lead to insights that are scientifically validated (or refuted), which then become part of the cybersecurity canon, to be spread through the literature and other formal and informal exchanges within the information technology community, as well as taught in the various schoolhouses. The Government can aid this process by empowering organizations such as the National Institute of Standards and Technology (NIST) and funding the various Advanced Research Project Agencies (ARPAs) and the National Science Foundation (NSF) to build a systematic body of knowledge.

These first two types of information sharing do not exacerbate the cybersecurity divide. The first should result in better software, which benefits everyone. The second should result in better cybersecurity practices, which also should benefit everyone, particularly those organizations that have at least one person who can think systematically about cybersecurity.

This now leaves the third type of information sharing, one that is specific to the characterization of threats and the impetus behind the legislation. It calls for organizations to report attacks and provide relevant details of these attacks, such as malware samples, attacker modus operandi, IP addresses, attack vectors, induced anomalies, social engineering methods, etc. These instances, in turn, are used to create a profile of specific threat actors and infer signatures of their activities, which, in turn, would be circulated to other organizations so that they can better prepare themselves, notably by putting such signatures into their intrusion prevention/detection systems. The appendix of the 2013 Mandiant report *(APT1: Exposing One of China's Cyber Espionage Units)*, for instance, was stuffed with many signatures that could be used by potential victims of APT1 (their name for a specific hacker group supported by China's Peoples Liberation Army) to recognize signs of threat activity infection. Although such signatures could, and in many cases, would also be supplemented by intelligence collection, the Classified nature of such additional material limits the number and type of machines on which they could reside.

The usefulness of threat-based information sharing rests on four assumptions about the nature of the threat itself. Such assumptions would have to be largely or totally true before the value of establishing an information-sharing apparatus can justify the effort to operate it, persuade organizations to contribute to it, and offset the residual risks to privacy that such information transfer may entail.

The first assumption is that a sufficient share of all serious attacks comes from specific black hat hacker groups and that each carry out enough attacks over a period of time so that their modus operandi can be characterized. Trivially, if every black hat hacker organization carried out just one attack, signatures derived from that one attack would inform no further attacks. In practice, each group must carry out enough attacks so those that are discovered can inform those that take place later on. Furthermore, for such signatures to be useful, there has to be time for the attack to be detected so that the signatures can be collected, shared, and inserted into the defensive systems of potential future victims while they are still useful. If all the attacks were bunched together in a short period, the information gathered from such attacks will not be gathered in time to be useful.

The second assumption is that each attacker group generates a consistent set of signatures that recur in multiple attacks (and that can be used reliably by defenders to distinguish their attacks from benign activity). To wit, hacker signatures have to resemble fingerprints. The APT1 group's attacks did have such characteristics (similarly, those that attacked Sony Pictures Entertainment in late 2014 used the same IP addresses as those who attacked South Korean banks and media firms in 2013). However, the possibilities of polymorphic malware (variations in the appearance of exploits) and fast-flux DNS (to permit shifting IP addresses) suggest that hackers have options for varying their signatures.

The third assumption is that these signatures are detectable by organizations interested in sharing. The average attacks by sophisticated and advanced threats remain undetected for a year—and those are only the ones that have been discovered. Most such attacks are discovered not by their victims but by third parties and, for the most part, only because the information taken from several victims is funneled through the same intermediate servers used to hold the exfiltrated data. If these servers are discovered, evidence from attacks on multiple victims can be picked up at the same time. Attackers who are sensitive to being caught can explore alternative ways to route the data they bring home.

The fourth assumption is that such signatures will not evolve (enough) over time—even if information sharing became so wide-spread that the failure to evolve would make it too hard for hacker groups to penetrate and compromise networks. Although Mandiant's publication of APT1 activities slowed the group's activities, it only took a few months before they were back in business using a new set of exploits and attack vectors, with brand-new signatures that had to be inferred.

An analogy may be drawn to the anti-virus industry. The major players—Symantec, McAfee, Kaspersky, and Microsoft—run very large information-gathering networks fed by inputs from customers as well as sensors that they have placed throughout the internet. But the anti-virus model has lost most of its viability over the past 5 years in the face of ever-shifting signatures and the practice of attackers testing malware against anti-virus suites before releasing them into the wild. Although threat-centric information-sharing deals with a broader range of indicators than anti-virus companies do, the same dynamic by which expensively-constructed measures beget relatively low-cost countermeasures argues against being terribly optimistic about the benefits from pushing a threat-centric information-sharing model.

This is not to say that threat-centric information sharing is useless. Not every black hat hacker group will be conscientious about altering its modus operandi, and there may be features of their signatures that are not obvious to themselves (and hence would likely persist for later detection). Forcing such groups to cluster their attacks or to use multiple attack vectors, including obfuscation techniques and grouping methods, resulting in new or altered signatures over time, means more work for them. Some attackers will drop out; others may not be able to attack as many organizations in a given period. So, the effort to gather signatures would not be completely wasted. Furthermore, even if threat-centric information sharing does not work, the efforts that organizations would have to make to understand what is going on in their networks in order to share information effectively would, as a side benefit, also help them protect themselves absent any information-sharing whatsoever.

Unfortunately, these recent efforts to promote a particular kind of information sharing have achieved the status of a panacea. They are absorbing a disproportional share of the legislative and elite media energy on the topic of cybersecurity. Many otherwise serious people assert that information sharing could have prevented many headline assaults on important networks. Yet, if one works through such attacks to understand if there were precedents that could have given us threat signatures, one often finds no good basis for such a belief. Quelling the Nation's cybersecurity problems is a complex, multi-faceted endeavor not subject to a silver bullet.

In sum, there is nothing wrong with information sharing. It should be encouraged. The President's proposal may well do so—in which case it deserves our support. But there is something wrong with assuming that it solves most, much less all, of the cybersecurity problem. It only addresses one facet of a very complex space. It is therefore highly questionable whether efforts to achieve information sharing deserve the political energy that they are currently taking up.

I appreciate the opportunity to discuss this important topic, and I look forward to your questions.

Mr. RATCLIFFE. Thank you, Dr. Libicki.

I now recognize myself for 5 minutes for questions.

Mr. Eggers, I'd like to start with you. In many respects, the Chamber of Commerce represents a single voice for stakeholders across many of the critical infrastructure sectors.

So, in that respect and capacity, can you address whether industry supports the sharing of cyber threat indicators through civilian portals, such as the NCCIC, with established and transparent privacy protections?

Mr. EGGERS. Congressman, thank you for that question.

I would say yes, we do. Just to give you an example, the NCCIC is a key portal through which businesses are sharing and will be sharing.

One thing I might add to that is we want businesses to be sharing with their trusted partners, whether it's DHS, FBI, Secret Service, Department of Energy, Treasury, you name it. I think what we want to see is a bill that gives them the ability to voluntarily share cyber threat indicators with associated protections with some flexibility in terms of sharing with Government. So it would be DHS and other entities.

Mr. RATCLIFFE. Thank you, Mr. Eggers.

Ms. Callahan, as I've listened to stakeholders across the spectrum here, including privacy groups, one of the recurring questions and concerns out there relates to the minimization of data, which you talked about in your testimony. As the former chief privacy officer at DHS, I know that you oversaw the processes and procedures on how DHS protects privacy when it comes to sharing cyber threat indicators.

Could you walk us through that in a little more detail? The measures that are in place at NCCIC to ensure that personal information is not shared with the Government.

Ms. CALLAHAN. Thank you for that question.

There are several steps and several procedures that DHS goes through, depending on how the threat is conveyed to Homeland Security, depending on how it's integrated and whether or not it's going to be shared.

As you mentioned, data minimization and only having the directly associated threat information is the key element both because it protects privacy better, of course, but, also, it helps identify what people should really be looking at if, indeed, information is shared and they don't have to go through the chaff.

At Homeland Security, there are multiple steps. First, when the threat comes in from the private sector, it can be reviewed by a human to go and look to see if it can be identified for what the specific threat is. It's then distilled down. It's very frequently often IP addresses, possibly URLs associated with it, and the very rate time associated with an email address.

It's distilled down to that kind of core element, and then it's compared to whether or not we know anything about this threat, what else is happening, where is it going.

To the extent that it's going to be shared, only that distilled element is going to be the purpose that it's shared. It also then, before sharing, is reviewed by a DHS privacy professional to confirm that minimization process.

Mr. RATCLIFFE. Terrific.

So, from your experience, what is your opinion on whether the privacy community supports the privacy protections that are currently in place at NCCIC?

Ms. CALLAHAN. I think the privacy community very specifically wants to have civilian control over information sharing, and that's an important tenet for the privacy community.

They also are very aware of the privacy protections that I described that are detailed in the multiple privacy impact assessments, privacy compliance reviews, and other public documents that have been detailed by the DHS privacy office.

In addition, Homeland Security has a subcommittee that is Classified at the Top Secret/SCI level that has had even more detailed briefings, and those include advocates and members of the community. So I think that, to the extent the privacy advocates can be comfortable with the privacy protections of information sharing, Homeland Security has met that.

Mr. RATCLIFFE. Terrific. Thank you.

Mr. Garcia, I think it's pretty well-known out there that the financial services sector has one of the most mature ISACs and is considered by many to be the gold standard for information sharing.

I think that we all need to be cognizant and careful from the committee standpoint not to break something that's currently working well. So with that in mind, a two-part question for you.

How would the President's legislative proposal affect the financial sector's current sharing of cyber threat information? Then, second, what recommendations do you have for other sectors, based on your experience, and what might be learned from the FS–ISAC model?

Mr. GARCIA. Thank you. That's a good question.

I think the President's proposal is almost explicitly with us not targeted at the financial services sector or trying to make any improvements to it. There is a recognition that we have established a fairly robust and mature information-sharing trust community and that the proposal would really try to get at many of those non-critical sectors that have not yet engaged in this level of information sharing.

So I would think that, on the edges, the proposal will help information sharing broadly and maybe the financial services as well, as long as the ISAO model is developed in a way that doesn't create too much confusion.

As I mentioned in my opening statement, we need to have a federated information-sharing capability, not a competitive one where one ISAO is trying to get more members and, therefore, is withholding information from other ISAOs. That's really important. If we have Balkanized or siloed information sharing, we are defeating the purpose of trying to get broader comprehensive situational awareness.

So for ISAOs standing up, I think we'll look forward to providing contributions to the standards development process for what constitutes a good information-sharing environment. I think key to that is we really started sharing robustly when we established a traffic light protocol—red, yellow, green, white—a cascade of different definitions of what information can be shared with whom and what information cannot be shared.

That is enforced. It's enforceable and it is enforced. That really cements the trust, that you know that, when you're going to share this information, that it is not going to be released anywhere else where it is not permitted. So that gives a contributor some level of confidence that their information is going to be protected, but it's also going to be used by other members of that community. So that is a key element.

The other element is having well-trained personnel who are able to analyze information and be able to assimilate and synthesize all the different feeds that are coming in and make sense of it in a way that can provide the users with some kind of a coherent guidance for what to do about it.

Mr. RATCLIFFE. Terrific. Thank you, Mr. Garcia.

Mr. Eggers, I want to come back to you for a second. As I mentioned before, I've had listening sessions with different groups and one of the things that we've learned is that, you know, liability protections are clearly going to be necessary to incentivize this information sharing.

Can you explain what types of liability protections are needed and why?

Mr. EGGERS. Sure. Let me just kind of give you a feel for the protections, in general, where that liability protection fits in.

So when we look at, let's say, something like the CISA bill—which, you know, unless there's maybe hiccups at an upcoming mark-up which could happen soon, we will support that bill. But I think about liability in terms of kind of four key protections. Right? So liability's probably the first and foremost liability. Right?

In the legislation, if you're acting within the terms of the bill, you will be getting liability protections for the ways in which you share with the private-sector and Government entities. There's a few nuances.

The second is regulatory protection, and the third is FOIA, and the fourth is anti-trust. So, if anything, I would mention that the liability protection probably sits at the top and is probably the most important one of the bunch, if you had to single one out.

Mr. RATCLIFFE. So expounding on that, why is private-to-private sharing so important——

Mr. EGGERS. Generally——

Mr. RATCLIFFE [continuing]. And the liability protections associated with that?

Mr. EGGERS. Sure. So within the construct of a voluntary program—right?—and I think it's important just to stress we're talking about a voluntary program where we're trying to create some legal certainty—businesses, when they are, let's say, fortunate to be able to identify, let's say, a breach, an incident, they've got those bits and pieces of technical data that they should share with business partners and the governments to provide everyone a better sense of real security.

But a lot of times what we hear from businesses is, "Hey, we want to do the right thing, but we're afraid that the information that we share will come back to bite us"—right?—"It will have a boomerang effect."

So they want protections to be able to share that with peers, and we encourage that. Right? So if there's some attacks that you know of that you can share with others so other folks can benefit, stop those attacks, that's a good thing. We want them to share with their business partners.

The FS–ISAC is a great example. But we also want businesses to share that narrow threat data with Government, too, so they can start to build a bigger picture and help others, Government and private sector.

Mr. RATCLIFFE. Terrific. Thank you, Mr. Eggers.

Dr. Libicki, in addition to threat and indicator information sharing, you mentioned two others: The sharing of software vulnerabilities with the software vendor and information sharing to improve cybersecurity practices.

In your opinion, what would you suggest as appropriate legislative actions to address or enable these two areas?

Mr. LIBICKI. I am not sure that you really need that much legislative action apart from, you know, appropriations authorization sort of information. Let me give you an example.

I think the total amount of money spent world-wide to reward people for finding vulnerabilities in software isn't much more than about $10 million a year. When you consider that, globally, $70 billion a year are spent on cybersecurity tools and services and if you believe that, in fact, reducing the number of vulnerabilities can make people safer, there is a certain amount of room to increase the amount of money being spent on finding vulnerabilities.

If I had to make a guess, I would say $10 million, which is not particularly large in the context of, say, DHS's total cybersecurity spending, could do a lot to encourage that kind of discovery.

In terms of the other type of information sharing, every particular attack in many ways can be associated with things that you could have done differently, better practices, best practices. Although we have a canon of best practices today, a lot of times our best practices can be described as belt and suspenders.

When you talk to CISOs who cannot afford both belts and suspenders, they want some sort of guidance as to which one is more important, how important is isolating systems, for instance, how important is multi-factor authentication, how important is training, how important are a lot of the various way that organizations can improve their cybersecurity.

A lot of the way that you learn how organizations can improve cybersecurity is to figure out when something got past these particular defenses.

So where you would want to put more resources in is a consolidated effort to try to assess the relative efficacy of various cybersecurity measures in the context in which they are used, and empowering NIST is one way to do that.

NIST tends not to want to make those sorts of, "Well, A is better than B decisions." But that's the kind of knowledge you're going to need for cybersecurity and, I think, in terms of R&D funding from NSF and the various ARPAs, is a way to help systematize this learning and collect the lessons from this learning.

Mr. RATCLIFFE. Thank you, Dr. Libicki.

Ms. Callahan, in listening sessions with privacy groups, I've heard that following the Fair Information Practice Principles is a key to protecting Americans' privacies.

In your opinion, what more can NCCIC do to increase transparency and ensure that these principles are followed?

Ms. CALLAHAN. Thank you, sir.

The Fair Information Practice Principles, or the FIPPs, are the cornerstone for any analysis of analyzing the privacy impact of certain considerations.

As you note, the NCCIC has applied the FIPPs in their processes. However, we can always improve. The NCCIC can also have—the transparency and the discussion of the effectiveness of information sharing I think could be a very valuable tool in light of the fact that, you know, we hear a lot about information sharing and how does it work? Mr. Garcia has some examples that I believe he'll share with you. But I think it's also important to understand why this information's being shared, what's happening to it, and where is it going.

Dr. Ozment's testimony earlier this month—or, I guess, in February does have some statistics, as does Under Secretary Spaulding's, but I think understanding the core elements would be an important factor.

The data minimization that I talked about and the procedures that NCCIC and CSNC go through are useful, and I think it wouldn't be—it would be good to again describe those in more detail and try to get some understanding.

Finally, the issue about security clearances is a difficult one, but at the same time I think we can get more information at an Unclassified level perhaps both to explain to the private-sector companies who are concerned as well as those advocates.

Thank you.

Mr. RATCLIFFE. Thank you.

So do you think that the sharing of cyber threat information should be exempt from FOIA?

Ms. CALLAHAN. I think that there are several factors to think about. Candidly, the information that I have seen that's been shared from private-sector companies or from DHS to other Government entities is difficult to parse if you're not a computer. You know, we're trying to identify the malware. We're trying to identify what the threat is specifically. From a FOIA perspective, to understand public policy issues I don't think is very helpful.

Furthermore, I certainly think that companies would be very reticent to share that information if, indeed, it was exposed to FOIA. I think it probably still meets under the FOIA qualifications of Exemption (b)(3).

So I don't know that we need necessarily new legislation on that, but I think that the FOIA exemption is both useful and getting the information wouldn't be all that helpful for the advocates themselves.

Mr. RATCLIFFE. Thank you, Ms. Callahan.

Mr. Eggers, what's your perspective on that question?

Mr. EGGERS. I think the exemption from—thank you—the exemption from disclosure is a fundamental part of any bill. Right? Businesses want to be sharing. We want them to share. They don't want to see their names necessarily in the headlines because they were trying to do the right thing.

Mr. RATCLIFFE. Terrific. Thank you.

Pleased to be joined by the gentleman from Florida, Mr. Clawson. I'd like to yield to him for questions.

Mr. CLAWSON. So you all had the good luck or bad luck of coming when it turns out to be a fly-out day, weather day, votes at the last second. I mean, you know, you had everything going against you. I wouldn't take personal offense to a bunch of folks not being here because it is an unusual day up here.

So I think I have a grasp on what we're trying to do and why we're trying to do it. But when I put myself, if I were a participating company, with so many different stakeholders, particularly if it was a multi-national, I don't know how you get this to work.

It feels like the right thing that the anti-trust blocks could get thrown out of the way by the Government. Liability insurance feels like a good start, too. But there still feels to be a lot of other obstacles that, if I were running my company, would give me lots of pause here.

There's a long list. Right? I mean, first of all, if I was and have operated in foreign countries and their governments wanted to do this to me, I know I'd just say no.

So the foreign stakeholders, including security holders, I think also makes this a lot more complicated, particularly in former Soviet Bloc countries, by the way, where they don't like Government involved in their IT systems. So the multi-national nature of stakeholders is the first thing that comes to mind.

The second thing that comes to mind is who's not going to participate. If you don't get a big block of people in my industry participating, I am not sure I'd want to.

The third thing I'd say is, "Isn't this going to slow me down?" More important, the very tool that you seem to be putting in place here might help the bad guys. Because if the Government does get in the middle almost at any level, it slows down, I think what the point is, disseminating data to the people that understand the malware as quickly as possible. So I could keep going on and on here.

So I kind of feel like I like the idea. The devil's in the details. If I were a business, you'd have to—you know, if I were running a business again, you'd have to lay out pretty clearly how we would get over some of these obstacles and me still keep my fiduciary responsibility to shareholders and the other stakeholders in the company.

When I hear that not everybody wants to participate, I say to myself, "Hmm. I can kind of understand that." Now, that's from a

48

non-IT guy, by the way. So you all know more about these things
than I do.

So take up where I've left off here. Am I on shaky ground in
terms of these kind of concerns or am I hitting on something that
you all have already anticipated and addressed prior to this in your
own studies and activities?

Mr. EGGERS. Congressman, if I may—and then others can join
me—let me try to come at your questions this way. They're very
good.

We're talking about information sharing, but one of the things
that's positive about the framework is you can be using the framework in any country, any province, any State. It's not mandatory.
It's voluntary.

So you don't have to come up specially-engineered cyber solutions
to comply with, let's say, regulations of each country. That would
not be good. That would be too costly even for big companies.

No. 2, information sharing, voluntary at least under the bill that
we are championing, the CISA bill currently in the Senate, at least
in draft form.

The information-sharing program we're looking to achieve is not
about surveillance. It's about sharing threat data from business-to-
business, business-to-government, and, hopefully, more and more
business-to-government so that can stop future attacks.

The Chamber—we were part of a letter that had——

Mr. CLAWSON. Can I interrupt just for a second?

Mr. EGGERS. Sure.

Mr. CLAWSON. Business-to-business I understand because, if the
attack hits here, let's get at the information to—by the way, even
my competitors. Right?—and so that they can be inoculated.

Mr. EGGERS. Uh-huh.

Mr. CLAWSON. Why Government?

Mr. EGGERS. We can't fight the bad guys without working together. When I think about the threats out there, it's not the way-
ward kid down the street that's having fun, maybe, breaking into
a computer system.

It's nation-states. It's people working on their behalf. It's super
criminal groups that I think Dr. Libicki points out is very costly.

So if we're going to—and I like to think of an information-sharing bill. It's trying to knock the bad guys off-balance. Right? We
need to push them off-balance. Right?

We're going to share and be more resilient, meaning industry
and Government. So we need to work together. We can't tackle nation-states or their proxies solo. We can't do it. So we need to work
together, and we need to do it smartly.

Mr. CLAWSON. Anybody else?

Mr. GARCIA. Sure. I agree with Mr. Eggers. I think, you know,
when you look at this very complicated world of cyber threats, the
industry has information that the Government does not have globally. We are located around the world. The Government has information that we do not have, Classified information, information
about nation-state activities. If we're not fusing that together, we're
really not getting a broad situational awareness. So we are not
where we should be.

The financial sector has been working closely with the Government to think about the ways to improve the bidirectional sharing of information between industry and Government, and the Government agencies recognize that internally they need to improve their processes or how do they process information within the Government and then what's the tear line, meaning what's the really critical information that can be sent to the private sector, leaving the sources and methods, which is Classified, out of it because we don't need that information.

So we're working through that process of trying to improve content and procedures. It isn't easy. Government is not—there's many agencies in the Government with different cultures and different ways of doing things. The same goes with the private sector. So——

Mr. CLAWSON. Am I right to say that the further down you push the actual activity, meaning Government becomes an abler, facilitator, as opposed to active participant, there's an inverse relationship so you'll get more—if less Government's involved on a direct basis, more companies will voluntarily sign up.

Am I right or wrong about that? You see, I know what I would feel. I know what I would think.

Mr. GARCIA. Yes. And——

Mr. CLAWSON. It feels like it will be quicker without the Government being a direct participant, and it feels like it will be, you know, less risky in a lot of ways if I am doing this peer-to-peer with protection of the Government as opposed to the Government being the clearinghouse and interpreter of the data.

Mr. GARCIA. We wouldn't look at the Government as a clearinghouse or interpreter either, but we do see them as a partner that—again, they can provide information we don't have and vice versa.

Yes, I think there will be companies and organizations out there that have less trust in working with the Government for the liability concerns that Mr. Eggers has articulated, but the same goes for company-to-company at times. We're dealing with competitors.

In the financial sector, it's not quite the same thing. We are all competitors in financial services. But when it comes to cybersecurity, we're all in it together. It is not a competitive issue. So we've gotten over that hurdle.

We understand that we have to proceed on the assumption that we are all under attack every day and we are all going to get hit at one point or another. So let's just come to the table with that and admit that. "Now, what are we going to do about it together?"

That's a trust relationship that has been building over time. Other industry sectors, not as much. Hopefully, this information-sharing and analysis organization model that the administration is trying to incentivize—maybe that will move other companies toward more trust-sharing models not just among themselves, but with the Government.

Mr. EGGERS. Congressman Clawson, if I may, let me add to that.

So you had mentioned about business interest and information sharing. The Chamber was one of about 35 associations representing—I don't know—back of the envelope, maybe 80 to 90 percent of the U.S. economy, stating that, "We need a good bill that clears away the legal policy underbrush, gives us certainty that, when we are sharing, we are protected."

Mr. CLAWSON. That's easy. Right? I mean, we all agree on that. I mean——

Mr. EGGERS. So one thing I might add, if I just may—you mentioned slowing things down—one thing that we are looking at—and the jury's still out with respect to the Executive Order on cyber information sharing, at least February 13—is the standards/best practices element of standing up more ISAOs—right?—or at least having organizations declare that they've self-certified it at a future date, that they are following certain standards/best practices.

One of the things that I think gives our members pause is not that you're going to be holding up an entity as a model for how to share well. What we're concerned about is, in that process of creating standards, highlighting best practices, that that could kind of gum up the information-sharing works.

Mr. CLAWSON. Right. Right. I mean, look, if I wanted to get a good laugh out of my employees, two lines I could say: "We're from corporate and we're here to help"—that always got a chuckle—or "We're from the Government and we're here to help."

You know, employee stakeholders have had long-time experience of hearing people say that and then it goes wrong on them. You know, that's the—for this to work, whether you're the Chamber or whoever we are, we would have to be able to convince the companies and, more importantly, the folks that are running the IT systems and the ERPs that both corporate and, you know, in this case, the Government, is really not going to slow them down.

I think clearing out the underbrush, as you say—I mean, that's a no-brainer. Right? I mean, take away the anti-trust and take away the liability and we're much more likely to share.

But then, after that, after many years in the private sector, this story gets more murky to me as, you know, good intentions where things could easily go wrong or not get enough companies to participate to make a difference.

I'm glad that the financial sector is in that position, but having been involved in other sectors, I am really pretty sure that they're not nearly as organized and that their industries, by the way, are not nearly as consolidated.

So, you know, in the financial—we still have got a lot of community banks left, but it's a much more consolidated environment than it is in a lot of other industries. Those unconsolidated environments are a different animal. I don't know if that's even a word or not. But that's a different animal than what you're talking about.

I don't want to take all the time here. But give me a reaction on whether I'm all wet here.

Mr. GARCIA. Well, you know, you can see where there are times when information sharing has slowed down, for example, when something is subject to law enforcement investigation. Okay?

Now no one can talk about it and you can't actually disseminate the facts about something that, if other potential victims had that information, they could shut down systems that might otherwise be attacked.

So, yeah, there will be situations where trying to engage with the Government is going to slow things down. There are other situations where it's going to speed things up.

For example, we had worked within the NCCIC cooperatively with DHS. There was a point-of-sale malware called Backoff that was infecting a lot of different retail outlets all over the country.

Actually coming together, we fused information that DHS had and what the financial sector had, and we made sense of what this point-of-sale malware was doing. We pushed out a joint product, basically said, "Here's the threat. Here's what it's trying to do. Here's what you need to do to fix it."

One of the participants in the activity had something like 50 stores located in 24 different States where they actually took that advice and they made the correction before it——

Mr. CLAWSON. Who identified the malware?

Mr. GARCIA. That could have been—I don't have the specifics. It could have been from law enforcement. Often law enforcement can find certain malware——

Mr. CLAWSON. Or an outside contractor to——

Mr. GARCIA. It comes from many different places. It can come from security companies who are on contract. It can come from law enforcement that's doing their own investigative forensics work. It can come from a member company of the FS–ISAC. It can come from an analyst at DHS or the intelligence community.

It's a matter of having that automated phone tree, if you will, where we can bring all of those sources of intelligence together and make sense of it. Sometimes it's slow. Sometimes it's faster.

We're trying to get ourselves to a point of more automated threat information sharing where we actually can take out some of the human dimension of having to pick up a phone and call somebody or send an email saying "Did you see what I just saw?" and, actually, the machines are recognizing these kinds of——

Mr. CLAWSON. Looking for patterns.

Mr. GARCIA. Yeah.

Mr. CLAWSON. Dr. Libicki.

Mr. LIBICKI. Yes.

Mr. CLAWSON. Anything to add?

Mr. LIBICKI. Yes. I want to add to some of the comments.

I think we have a common stake in better cybersecurity. Okay? In a world in which, say, one bank is subject to an attack that causes people to lose trust in the bank, their neighbor across the street isn't going to be better off. In many ways, they're going to be worse off.

The attack that makes people wonder if they can give a credit card to one merchant isn't going to necessarily have them running to another merchant. It's going to complicate the response of everybody who wants to use credit cards in commerce. For that reason, there is going to be a common interest in information security, in cybersecurity, and improving it across the lot.

To a large extent we shouldn't forget that the Government organizations themselves have an interest in their own cybersecurity and there's information on best practices, on how to make good decisions, that they can learn from the rest of the economy, or the benefits that they get from closing vulnerabilities in software used in business also helps the Government organizations preserve their own systems, preserve their own confidentiality in their systems and——

Mr. CLAWSON. That's a good point.

Mr. LIBICKI [continuing]. Authentication.

Mr. CLAWSON. That's a good point.

Ms. CALLAHAN. If I may, sir, just to follow up, I think about information sharing both among the companies and, also, with and from the Government as kind of three-dimensional chess. You need to know where each of the different elements are, as Mr. Garcia and Dr. Libicki talked about, and you may not have the complete picture unless you get all of the information.

I completely agree with you that you don't want the Government in your business dealing with what the threat is itself, but you do want to share the information that you've figured out or maybe a contractor figured out or maybe the Government figured out.

So it's to share the information as broadly as possible, but not to have the Government come and, you know, deal with the information or address the cyber threat unless it's a critical scenario.

Mr. EGGERS. Congressman, if I may just add a quick point, one thing I think about or at least our members think about in terms of getting from Point A to Point B, A to Z, on an information-sharing bill, a bill that clears both Chambers and, hopefully, gets to the President's desk this year, is, even though it's important to protect privacy, that we not lose sight of the burdens that we could place on small and mid-sized businesses to scrub personal information.

Those kinds of provisions will be in a bill, but I want to make sure that we not go too far that we're essentially, from a practical standpoint, having the small and mid-sized guys sit on the sidelines because they feel like they can't scrub personal information adequately or do it at least under the terms of any future bill.

Mr. CLAWSON. Boy, that's a tough balance. I mean, I thought about this all day. We talked about it with our team. With small businesses that don't have a lot of dedicated resources and often outsource anything of any complexity with regards to—I mean, they even outsource their own ERP system. Right?

You know, to get a bill which will convince those folks to participate in a voluntary program that could make their life more difficult and still get the bill through—because you're going to have folks like me that are going to say, "I'm just not fond of the Government being in my cell or in my ERP, either one, really."

That's going to be a neat trick. Right? I mean, that just doesn't feel like it will be easy to do. I'm not trying to be critical. It just feels like a mountain to climb here to get it just right where you don't make it so onerous that no one signs up. But you have got to have something that has enough impact to get the bill passed.

Am I making sense?

Mr. EGGERS. Yes. One quick brief note on that is, when I say small and mid-sized guys just generically, I'm thinking in a lot of ways some of the supply chain elements of, let's say, a bigger firm.

If those smaller companies are hacked, we want them to have the confidence that they report, let's say, to the bigger company and a lot of times the Government won't necessarily have to be in their systems.

What they will be doing is sharing those technical bits and pieces of information that the bigger company can use and, let's say, law enforcement can use to build a case against folks probably overseas.

Mr. CLAWSON. Well, if I can help you—I mean, I'm playing devil's advocate here, obviously. But I'm doing it because I'm trying to—you know, I hope this works. I don't want it to fail. We want it to work.

Mr. EGGERS. Agreed.

Mr. CLAWSON. So I think the more front-end conversations you have like this one—and I know you're doing that every day with people that are out there—the better your chances of getting people to participate.

Because, if they don't come around, we're dead. Right? I mean, if it's a voluntary program and no one signs up, then it's not going to do us much good.

Ms. CALLAHAN. I think, for the small and medium-sized businesses, the automated sharing that Mr. Garcia talked about can really help facilitate that. Therefore, the more people can participate, the bigger the pie, so to speak, the more you can share, the less burden it is on the small and medium-sized enterprises.

Mr. CLAWSON. I yield back.

Thank you, everybody, for your patience with me.

Mr. RATCLIFFE. I thank the gentleman.

I agree with the gentleman that weather has definitely affected attendance today. But I know that my colleagues on both sides of the aisle see this as a critically important issue, as evidenced by the fact that a number of them were with me earlier this morning and with the Chairman, touring the NCCIC.

So, with that, I am very grateful to the witnesses for their valuable testimony. I know that it will inform this committee as we move forward.

I thank my colleague for his questions.

The Members of the committee may have some additional questions for witnesses, and we'll ask them to respond to these in writing. Pursuant to committee rule 7(e), the hearing record will be held open for 10 days.

Without objection, the subcommittee stands adjourned.

[Whereupon, at 4:08 p.m., the subcommittee was adjourned.]

○